D0746139

Authority and the Individual

'Russell has rarely written more lucidly, lightly and directly'

The Spectator

Routledge Classics contains the very best of Routledge publishing over the past century or so, books that have, by popular consent, become established as classics in their field. Drawing on a fantastic heritage of innovative writing published by Routledge and its associated imprints, this series makes available in attractive, affordable form some of the most important works of modern times.

For a complete list of titles visit
www.routledge.com/classics

Bertrand
Russell

Authority and the Individual

 London and New York

First published 1949

First published in the Routledge Classics in 2010
by Routledge
2 Park Square, Milton Park, Abingdon, Oxon OX14 4RN

Simultaneously published in the USA and Canada
by Routledge
711 Third Avenue, New York, NY 10017, USA

Routledge is an imprint of the Taylor & Francis Group, an informa business

© 2010 The Bertrand Russell Peace Foundation Ltd

Introduction © 1995 Kirk Willis

Typeset in Joanna by RefineCatch Limited, Bungay, Suffolk

British Library Cataloguing in Publication Data
A catalogue record for this book is available from the British Library

Library of Congress Cataloging-in-Publication Data
A catalog record for this book has been requested

ISBN10: 0–415–48733–1
ISBN10: 0–203–86487–5 (ebk)

ISBN13: 978–0–415–48733–7
ISBN13: 978–0–203–86487–6 (ebk)

CONTENTS

PREFATORY NOTE

In the preparation of these lectures I have had the benefit of vital assistance by my wife, Patricia Russell, not only as regards details, but as regards the general ideas and their application to the circumstances of the present day.

Bertrand Russell

INTRODUCTION

For nearly fifty years, the Reith Lectures have enjoyed a distinguished place in the cultural life of modern Britain. Traditionally delivered deep in the autumn and early winter, they honour the founding Director of the BBC, John Reith. Proud, imperious, and vindictive, Reith was an autocratic administrator and formidable personality who succeeded brilliantly both in bruising the sensibilities of subordinates and overseers alike and in creating one of Britain's most admired and durable institutions. True to Reith's insistence that the BBC make available to its audience the most eminent of speakers on the most wide-ranging of subjects, the Reith lecturers have been chosen for the breadth of their interests, the mastery of their subjects, and the ease of their ability to make difficult issues intelligible to a broad audience. Since 1948, the British public has therefore been enlightened by anthropologists and zoologists, astronomers and diplomats, art historians and economists, theologians and tycoons.

That the Reith Lectures would become so enduring an institution was certainly the ambition – if not honestly the expectation – of their creator: the Board of Governors of the BBC. To the Board, in the difficult early months of post-war readjustment, the establishment of the lectures was intended not merely to honour Reith but, more importantly, to contribute to the understanding of a radically different world – a world of Labour governments and atomic energy, of European reconstruction and superpower rivalry, of imperialistic challenges and economic degradation Their ambition, indeed, was to create an annual radio version of the Gifford Lectures – an accessible statement, aimed at a wide audience, by some of Britain's most original thinkers and creative researchers. To inaugurate the series, and thereby both to set the tone and to establish the credentials of the lectures, the Board invited Britain's most celebrated public intellectual – Bertrand Russell.

Such a position in the good graces of the cultural and intellectual elite of twentieth-century Britain was at once a pleasure and a novelty for Russell. Indeed, the decade immediately after the end of the Second World War marked a rare moment of public respectability for Russell, whose reputation – scholarly, political, and personal – had fluctuated (and would continue to fluctuate) wildly over the course of his extraordinarily long life. Born in 1872 into one of the most eminent and secure families of Britain's Whig aristocracy, Russell had made his intellectual reputation in the two decades before the outbreak of the Great War. Ensconced in a Cambridge lectureship in logic and the philosophy of mathematics created especially for him, he had enjoyed two decades of uninterrupted intellectual achievement. With works ranging from *An Essay on the Foundations of Geometry* (1897), to *A Critical Exposition of the Philosophy of Leibniz* (1900), to *The Principles of Mathematics* (1903), to *The Problems of Philosophy* (1912), to *Principia Mathematica* (3 vols, 1910–13), to over thirty major articles in British, French, Italian, and American journals, Russell had won renown not simply as a formidable logician possessed of a rare technical sophistication and an even rarer

stylistic virtuosity but as the chief proponent of a new and powerful technique of intellectual discourse – analytic philosophy. On
the eve of the First World War, indeed, Russell had been
indisputably the most celebrated and influential philosopher in
the English-speaking world.

The outbreak of the Great War, however, had transformed
Russell's life; if his philosophical work had brought him fame,
the Great War made him notorious. Although never an arche-
typically cloistered Cambridge don – he had been active in the
tariff reform campaign in 1903 and the women's suffrage
movement from 1907 and had begun an aborted campaign for
Parliament in 1910 – Russell had none the less not been a public
man. But as Britain marched remorselessly to war in the summer
of 1914, Russell threw himself first into the neutrality campaign
and then into the anti-war movement – speaking, writing,
organizing, and counselling. No pacifist, Russell passionately
believed that this particular war – not all war – was a mistake;
indeed, it offended his every political instinct and moral principle. And as the war lengthened and Britain's commitment
extended, Russell's opposition had sharpened – to mistreatment
of conscientious objectors, to the suppression of civil liberties,
and to the wastefulness of British commanders. This opposition –
strident, unrelenting, and bitterly unpopular – was the defining
experience of Russell's life; not merely did emotions run so high
on all sides that Russell alienated friends, exasperated allies, and
infuriated authorities, but his appreciation that the war was
genuinely popular with the vast majority of his fellow subjects at
once appalled and captivated him. To explain that popularity – to
account for the belligerence and xenophobia of the British public and to fathom their susceptibility to the exaggerations of the
Press lords and their indifference to the centralizing tendencies
of their government – had become Russell's central intellectual
and political task in the years after 1918.

The inter-war years had therefore seen a very different Russell devoted to a very different sort of work. Self-consciously determined to become the Voltaire of the twentieth century, Russell had engaged directly – and often in a very public manner – with an astonishing range of issues in an effort to reconstruct society and regenerate individuals so as to prevent a second military catastrophe. Lecturing, writing, teaching, and travelling, Russell sent forth not solitary spies but battalions of words to do battle – on political theory (*Roads to Freedom* (1918) and *Power* (1938)), on economic change (*The Prospects of Industrial Civilization* (1923)), on history (*Freedom and Organization 1814–1914* (1934)), on the future of Asia (*The Problem of China* (1922)), on Russia (*The Practice and Theory of Bolshevism* (1920)), on education (*On Education* (1926) and *Education and the Social Order* (1932)), on marriage and sexuality (*Marriage and Morals* (1929)), on mathematics (*An Introduction to Mathematical Philosophy* (1919)), on fascism (*Which Way to Peace?* (1936)), on science (*The ABC of Atoms* (1923), *Icarus* (1924), *The ABC of Relativity* (1925), and *The Scientific Outlook* (1931)), on popular philosophy (*Analysis of Mind* (1921) and *Outline of Philosophy* (1927)), and on religion (*What I Believe* (1925)). Although much of this writing and most of the journalism which supplemented it proved evanescent, it none the less reached a wide audience and served to heighten Russell's notoriety still further; indeed, for all that his liberal views on religion, ethics, and sexuality had attracted the young, independent, and free-thinking, they had also offended the comfortable, conforming, and established.

The outbreak of the Second World War had found Russell teaching in America. Eager to return to Britain and embroiled in controversy over his popular writings, Russell had been prohibited from returning by a British government all too willing to remember his earlier antiwar opinions and activities but not to believe his current – and quite genuine – protestations of support for this conflict against Nazi Germany and Fascist Italy. He had therefore remained in America until the summer of 1944 – writing, lecturing, teaching, and preparing the mammoth manuscript of what would become his most widely-read book, *History of Western Philosophy* (1945).

Russell had returned not simply to England but to Cambridge, and not merely to Cambridge but to Trinity College – where he had been an undergraduate in the 1890s and a don in the 1910s, and from which he had been driven in 1916 by a governing body unable to tolerate his anti-war opinions. Invited by his old undergraduate friend and the current Master of Trinity, G. M. Trevelyan, Russell had recognized and happily accepted the fellowship offered him for what it was – an amends for earlier wrongs and a testimony to his continued standing as one of the preeminent philosophers of the twentieth century. To return to England, to Trinity, to Newton's own rooms in the immediate aftermath of the invasion of France and final stages of the defeat of Germany meant much to Russell, who had left the Britain of the late 1930s sour and pessimistic – angry at the evasions of British foreign and defence policies, dismayed at the incapacity and unwillingness of National governments to relieve pervasive social and economic misery, and of two minds whether to raise his children as British subjects. But by 1944 that low, dishonest decade had passed, and the quick succession of Allied victory, Labour triumph, and publishing success of the *History of Western Philosophy* all combined to lift Russell's spirits and to allow his natural resilience and optimism to blossom forth lavishly.

At Trinity Russell had been received warmly by old friends and those few students not in military service. With the war's end, followed hard by Labour's victory and the *History*'s success, Russell found himself lionized. Not expected by the college authorities either to teach or to lecture, Russell threw himself into both with a vigour and enthusiasm astonishing in a man of seventy-two. To his delight, he won a ready and receptive audience. Introductory lecture courses on such subjects as ethics, epistemology, and the fundamentals of philosophy filled the largest lecture rooms Cambridge possessed to overflowing.

Derived in their essentials from his *History of Western Philosophy* (itself largely a compilation of American lectures), Russell's lectures were memorable performances – lucid, witty, irreverent, full of sweeping themes and picturesque asides, and delivered with a brio that managed at one to enthrall his audience and to incarnate the moral seriousness and intellectual grandeur of philosophical study. To his listeners at Cambridge and readers across the English-speaking world, Russell – the grandson of Lord John Russell and godchild of John Stuart Mill – quickly came to seem not merely a living connection with Britain's political and cultural greatness, but the robust embodiment of a western culture that had prevailed over the evils of fascism and vanquished the horrors of nazism. Russell had thus come to be seen – and to see himself – not as a gadfly or a renegade but as an ornament of a triumphant Britain now determined to build a wholly new society on the sturdy and enduring foundations of the past.

An appreciation of Russell's unique standing as well as of his new mellowness soon spread far beyond Cambridge, driven in large measure by the remarkable sales of the *History of Western Philosophy* – sales limited only by the shortage of paper in an economically bereft Britain. Russell therefore soon found himself a favourite lecturer of the British Council and, unimaginably to anyone alive in 1916, of the Foreign Office; at their behest, Russell travelled in the next years to Switzerland, Norway, Germany, and France to lecture on such topics as 'Culture and the State' and 'Ethics and Power'.

It was in this context of renewed respectability that the BBC discovered Russell. Firmly beyond their pale in the 1920s and 1930s, Russell had been shunned by Reith and his successors as a dangerous radical bristling with extreme opinions. Now apparently more moderate and trustworthy, he was invited to appear on the popular Brains Trust programme late in 1944. So successful did his appearance prove to be, that he was almost immediately asked to broadcast on 'The Future of Civilization' and then to debate such worthies as J. B. S. Haldane and Frederick Copleston. To the delight of BBC engineers and directors, Russell proved to be an almost model broadcaster – punctual, informed, lively, and provocative without being outrageous. By the end of 1946 it seemed the BBC could not get enough of him, and in January 1947 Russell complained of overwork 'as the BBC has developed a passion for me'.[1] It was therefore out of this popularity – both within Broadcasting House and without – that he was invited to be the inaugural Reith lecturer.

The lectures were given as six half-hour talks on successive Sunday evenings beginning on Boxing Day 1948. Written out completely beforehand and delivered in Russell's somewhat reedy yet unnervingly precise voice, they were devoted to a theme about which he and other liberal thinkers had thought long and hard: how is it possible to 'combine that degree of individual initiative which is necessary for progress with the degree of social cohesion that is necessary for survival.' Russell's lectures, that is, were neither a progress report drawn from an ongoing programme of research (as would be those of J. Z. Young in 1950 and Peter Medawar in 1959) nor a culminating statement of a lifetime's academic or professional work (as would be those of Bernard Lovell in 1958 and Alastair Buchan in 1973). They were, rather, the product of a full forty years of reflection about the relations of individuals and the state and about the evolving forms power and authority have taken in the twentieth century. Russell's lectures, that is, neither summarized current research, nor presented new conclusions, nor laid out a new line of inquiry. Instead, they distilled his earlier thinking, drew together themes he had discussed in the inter-war years, meditated on the legacies of totalitarian states (both vanquished and extant), and explained the challenges liberal societies faced in the remaining decades of the twentieth century.

As Russell confessed early in his lectures, questions concerning

the proper balance of state power ('authority') and human freedom ('the individual') have been at the heart of liberal political
theory since at least the seventeenth century. But Russell's
discussion of them in 1948 possessed an extra immediacy – an
immediacy that helps, in large measure, to account for their
quite remarkable popularity. Within Britain itself, as his listeners
were well aware, the advent of the Attlee Government in 1945
had set Britain on a dramatic new course – of nationalized industries and educational reform, of social insurance and the
National Health Service – which cumulatively entailed a sweeping extension of state authority over nearly every aspect of
British society. The implications of that extension – for social
cohesion, individual initiative, and personal responsibility – were
at the very heart of an intense, often bitter national debate – a
debate not merely over the details of specific pieces of legislation
but also over the values, behaviour, and expectations of each and
every British subject. Beyond Britain, moreover, the establishment of Soviet-style regimes in eastern Europe in the late 1940s
also prompted intense discussion about the nature of totalitarian
states and the dangers of increased state control, discussion to
which Arthur Koestler, Karl Popper, and George Orwell, among
others, would contribute so memorably. In addressing himself to
the theme of 'authority and the individual' Russell was therefore
not merely presenting the fruits of his own accumulated reflection but also joining an impassioned and compelling discussion
with the widest possible ramifications.

To read *Authority and the Individual* is to discover Russell at his
most characteristic and persuasive – lucid, intelligent, serious-
minded but not solemn, and concerned not with the presentation of detailed schemes for world government, local government
reform, or charters of liberty, but with the clearing away of
confusions and the articulation of first principles. One discovers
Russell, as the precise logician and accomplished teacher that he
was, explaining to us the nature of the questions that must be

asked before any such schemes can sensibly be fashioned. Russell thus leads his readers through such perennial, if essential, topics as the formation and purpose of society, the nature and function of justice, the scope of education and evolution of moral codes, and the mechanisms of social, economic, and intellectual progress. He does so, moreover, with a clear eye on contemporary realities – on technological advances that have at once enhanced the state's capacity for surveillance and enforcement and diminished the individual's ability to withstand that power, on transformations in warfare that promise atomic armageddon as a consequence of misdirected aggression, and on innovations in the arts of advertising, propaganda, and media which threaten to weaken our ability and willingness to think for ourselves. By the end of his sixth lecture Russell has thus provided us with an insightful examination of the intellectual, political, and moral challenges confronting contemporary western society, a stringent warning of the encroaching power of authority in all its guises, and a stirring reaffirmation of human liberty both as an end in itself and as a means to further human progress.

By any standard the first Reith Lectures were a triumphant success. To be sure, John Reith – never an easy man to please – complained that Russell had spoken 'far too quickly' and in 'a bad voice'.[2] Critics and listeners, however, proved far more admiring. Old friends, ancient adversaries, and unknown admirers wrote to Russell in the scores, nearly all of them sharing T. S. Eliot's judgement that Russell was 'one of the few living authors who can write English prose' and endorsing The Times's assessment that the talks marked 'another landmark in broadcasting history'.[3] When a very slightly amended version of the lectures appeared in book form as Authority and the Individual in the late spring of 1949, it won both critical approval and wide sales, reaching 500 copies a week long into the summer.

As such a gratifying critical reception made plain, Authority and the Individual was a timely and powerful tract for its times, vindicating the BBC's selection and confirming Russell's newly-found respectability. In its forceful and articulate presentation of the inescapable tensions between the claims of authority and requirements of liberty, moreover, it has only gained in poignancy as our troubled century draws to its close. In the scale of its ambition, in the wisdom of its analysis, and in the inspiration of its conclusions, *Authority and the Individual* still speaks to us eloquently and forcefully.

Kirk Willis, University of Georgia

NOTES

1   Quoted in Ronald W. Clark, *The Life of Bertrand Russell* (London, 1975), p. 496.
2   Charles Stuart, ed., *The Reith Diaries* (London, 1975), p. 464.
3   T. S. Eliot to Russell, 10 June 1949, in *The Autobiography of Bertrand Russell 1944–1967* (London, 1969), p. 52. The quotation from *The Times* is cited in Caroline Moorehead, *Bertrand Russell* (London, 1992), p. 460.

Lecture 1

SOCIAL COHESION AND HUMAN NATURE

The fundamental problem I propose to consider in these lectures is this: how can we combine that degree of individual initiative which is necessary for progress with the degree of social cohesion that is necessary for survival? I shall begin with the impulses in human nature that make social co-operation possible. I shall examine first the forms that these impulses took in very primitive communities, and then the adaptations that were brought about by the gradually changing social organisations of advancing civilisation. I shall next consider the extent and intensity of social cohesion in various times and places, leading up to the communities of the present day and the possibilities of further development in the not very distant future. After this discussion of the forces that hold society together I shall take up the other side of the life of Man in communities, namely, individual initiative, showing the part that it has played in various phases of human evolution, the part that it plays at the present day, and the future possibilities of too much or too little initiative in individuals and groups. I shall then go on to one of the basic problems of our times, namely, the conflict which modern technique has introduced between organisation and human nature, or, to put the matter in another way, the divorce of the economic motive from the impulses of creation and possession. Having stated this problem, I shall examine what can be done towards its solution, and finally I shall consider as a matter of ethics the whole relation of individual thought and effort and imagination to the authority of the community.

In all social animals, including Man, co-operation and the unity of a group has some foundation in instinct. This is most complete in ants and bees, which apparently are never tempted to anti-social actions and never deviate from devotion to the nest or the hive. Up to a point we may admire this unswerving devotion to public duty, but it has its drawbacks; ants and bees do not produce great works of art, or make scientific discoveries, or found religions teaching that all ants are sisters. Their social life, in fact, is mechanical, precise and static. We are willing that human life shall have an element of turbulence if thereby we can escape such evolutionary stagnation.

Early Man was a weak and rare species whose survival at first was precarious. At some period his ancestors came down from the trees and lost the advantage of prehensile toes, but gained the advantage of arms and hands. By these changes they acquired the advantage of no longer having to live in forests, but on the other hand the open spaces into which they spread provided a less abundant nourishment than they had enjoyed in the tropical jungles of Africa. Sir Arthur Keith estimates that primitive Man required two square miles of territory per individual to supply him with food, and some other authorities place the amount of territory required even higher. Judging by the anthropoid apes, and by the most primitive communities that have survived into modern times, early man must have lived in small groups not very much larger than families – groups which, at a guess, we may put at, say, between fifty and a hundred individuals. Within each group there seems to have been a considerable amount of co-operation, but towards all other groups of the same species there was hostility whenever contact occurred. So long as Man remained rare, contact with other groups could be occasional, and, at most times, not very important. Each group had its own territory, and conflicts would only occur at the frontiers. In those early times marriage appears to have been confined to the group, so that there must have been a very great deal of inbreeding, and varieties, however originating, would tend to be perpetuated. If a group increased in numbers to the point where its existing territory was insufficient, it would be likely to come into conflict with some neighbouring group, and in such conflict any biological advantage which one inbreeding group had acquired over the other might be expected to give it the victory, and therefore to perpetuate its beneficial variation. All this has been very convincingly set forth by Sir Arthur Keith. It is obvious that our early and barely human ancestors cannot have been acting on a thought-out and deliberate policy, but must have been prompted by an instinctive mechanism – the dual mechanism of friendship within the tribe and hostility to all others. As the primitive tribe was so small, each individual would know intimately each other individual, so that friendly feeling would be co-extensive with acquaintanceship.

The strongest and most instinctively compelling of social groups was, and still is, the family. The family is necessitated among human beings by the great length of infancy, and by the fact that the mother of young infants is seriously handicapped in the work of food gathering. It was this circumstance that with human beings, as with most species of birds, made the father an essential member of the family group. This must have led to a division of labour in which the men hunted while the women stayed at home. The transition from the family to the small tribe was presumably biologically connected with the fact that hunting could be more efficient if it was co-operative, and from a very early time the cohesion of the tribe must have been increased and developed by conflicts with other tribes.

The remains that have been discovered of early men and half-men are now sufficiently numerous to give a fairly clear picture of the stages in evolution, from the most advanced anthropoid apes to the most primitive human beings. The earliest indubitably human remains that have been discovered so far are estimated to belong to a period about one million years ago, but for several million years before that time there seem to have been anthropoids that lived on the ground and not in trees. The most distinctive feature by which the evolutionary status of these early ancestors is fixed is the size of the brain, which increased fairly rapidly until it reached about its present capacity, but has now been virtually stationary for hundreds of thousands of years. During these hundreds of thousands of years Man has improved in knowledge, in acquired skill, and in social organisation, but not, so far as can be judged, in congenital intellectual capacity. That purely biological advance, so far as it can be estimated from bones, was completed a long time ago. It is to be supposed accordingly that our congenital mental equipment, as opposed to what we learn, is not so very different from that of Paleolithic Man. We have still, it would seem, the instincts which led men, before their behaviour had become deliberate, to live in small tribes, with a sharp antithesis of internal friendship and external hostility. The changes that have come since those early times have had to depend for their driving force partly upon this primitive basis of instinct, and partly upon a sometimes barely conscious sense of collective self-interest. One of the things that cause stress and strain in human social life is that it is possible, up to a point, to become aware of rational grounds for a behaviour not prompted by natural instinct. But when such behaviour strains natural instinct too severely nature takes her revenge by producing either listlessness or destructiveness, either of which may cause a structure inspired by reason to break down.

Social cohesion, which started with loyalty to a group reinforced by the fear of enemies, grew by processes partly natural and partly deliberate until it reached the vast conglomerations that we now know as nations. To these processes various forces contributed. At a very early stage loyalty to a group must have been reinforced by loyalty to a leader. In a large tribe the chief or king may be known to everybody even when private individuals are often strangers to each other. In this way, personal as opposed to tribal loyalty makes possible an increase in the size of the group without doing violence to instinct.

At a certain stage a further development took place. Wars, which originally were wars of extermination, gradually became – at least in part – wars of conquest; the vanquished, instead of being put to death, were made slaves and compelled to labour for their conquerors. When this happened there came to be two sorts of people within a community, namely, the original members who alone were free, and were the repositories of the tribal spirit, and the subjects who obeyed from fear, not from instinctive loyalty. Nineveh and Babylon ruled over vast territories, not because their subjects had any instinctive sense of social cohesion with the dominant city, but solely because of the terror inspired by its prowess in war. From those early days down to modern times war has been the chief engine in enlarging the size of communities, and fear has increasingly replaced tribal solidarity as a source of social cohesion. This change was not confined to large communities; it occurred, for example, in Sparta, where the free citizens were a small minority, while the Helots were unmercifully suppressed. Sparta was praised throughout antiquity for its admirable social cohesion, but it was a cohesion which never attempted to embrace the whole population, except in so far as terror compelled outward loyalty.

At a later stage in the development of civilisation, a new kind of loyalty began to be developed; a loyalty based not on territorial affinity or similarity of race, but on identity of creed. So far as the West is concerned this seems to have originated with the Orphic communities, which admitted slaves on equal terms. Apart from them religion in antiquity was so closely associated with government that groups of co-religionists were broadly identical with the groups that had grown up on the old biological basis. But identity of creed has gradually become a stronger and stronger force. Its military strength was first displayed by Islam in the conquests of the seventh and eighth centuries. It supplied the moving force in the Crusades and in the wars of religion. In the sixteenth century theological loyalties very often outweighed those of nationality: English Catholics often sided with Spain, French Huguenots with England. In our own day two widespread creeds embrace the loyalty of a very large part of mankind. One of these, the creed of Communism, has the advantage of intense fanaticism and embodiment in a Sacred Book. The other, less definite, is nevertheless potent – it may be called 'The American Way of Life'. America, formed by immigration from many different countries, has no biological unity, but it has a unity quite as strong as that of European nations. As Abraham Lincoln said, it is 'dedicated to a proposition'. Immigrants into America often suffer from nostalgia for Europe, but their children, for the most part, consider the American way of life preferable to that of the Old World, and believe firmly that it would be for the good of mankind if this way of life became universal. Both in America and in Russia unity of creed and national unity have coalesced, and have thereby acquired a new strength, but these rival creeds have an attraction which transcends their national boundaries.

Modern loyalty to the vast groups of our time, in so far as it is strong and subjectively satisfying, makes use still of the old psychological mechanism evolved in the days of small tribes. Congenital human nature, as opposed to what is made of it by schools and religions, by propaganda and economic organisations, has not changed much since the time when men first began to have brains of the size to which we are accustomed. Instinctively we divide mankind into friends and foes – friends, towards whom we have the morality of co-operation; foes, towards whom we have that of competition. But this division is constantly changing; at one moment a man hates his business competitor, at another, when both are threatened by Socialism or by an external enemy, he suddenly begins to view him as a brother. Always when we pass beyond the limits of the family it is the external enemy which supplies the cohesive force. In times of safety we can afford to hate our neighbour, but in times of danger we must love him. People do not, at most times, love those whom they find sitting next to them in a bus, but during the blitz they did.

It is this that makes the difficulty of devising means of worldwide unity. A world state, if it were firmly established, would have no enemies to fear, and would therefore be in danger of breaking down through lack of cohesive force. Two great religions – Buddhism and Christianity – have sought to extend to the whole human race the co-operative feeling that is spontaneous towards fellow tribesmen. They have preached the brotherhood of Man, showing by the use of the word 'brotherhood' that they are attempting to extend beyond its natural bounds an emotional attitude which, in its origin, is biological. If we are all children of God, then we are all one family. But in practice those who in theory adopted this creed have always felt that those who did not adopt it were not children of God but children of Satan, and the old mechanism of hatred of those outside the tribe has returned, giving added vigour to the creed, but in a direction which diverted it from its original purpose. Religion, morality, economic self-interest, the mere pursuit of biological survival, all supply to our intelligence unanswerable arguments in favour of world-wide cooperation, but the old instincts that have come down to us from our tribal ancestors rise up in indignation, feeling that life would lose its savour if there were no one to hate, that anyone who could have loved such a scoundrel as so-and-so would be a worm, that struggle is the law of life, and that in a world where we all loved one another there would be nothing to live for. If the unification of mankind is ever to be realised, it will be necessary to find ways of circumventing our largely unconscious primitive ferocity, partly by establishing a reign of law, and partly by finding innocent outlets for our competitive instincts.

This is not an easy problem, and it is one which cannot be solved by morality alone. Psycho-analysis, though no doubt it has its exaggerations, and even perhaps absurdities, has taught us a great deal that is true and valuable. It is an old saying that even if you expel nature with a pitchfork it will still come back, but psycho-analysis has supplied the commentary to this text. We now know that a life which goes excessively against natural impulse is one which is likely to involve effects of strain that may be quite as bad as indulgence in forbidden impulses would have been. People who live a life which is unnatural beyond a point are likely to be filled with envy, malice and all uncharitableness. They may develop strains of cruelty, or, on the other hand, they may so completely lose all joy in life that they have no longer any capacity for effort. This latter result has been observed among savages brought suddenly in contact with modern civilisation. Anthropologists have described how Papuan head hunters, deprived by white authority of their habitual sport, lose all zest, and are no longer able to be interested in anything. I do not wish to infer that they should have been allowed to go on hunting heads, but I do mean that it would have been worth while if psychologists had taken some trouble to find some innocent substitute activity. Civilised Man everywhere is, to some degree, in the position of the Papuan victims of virtue. We have all kinds of aggressive impulses, and also creative impulses, which society forbids us to indulge, and the alternatives that it supplies in the shape of football matches and all-in wrestling are hardly adequate. Anyone who hopes that in time it may be possible to abolish war should give serious thought to the problem of satisfying harmlessly the instincts that we inherit from long generations of savages. For my part I find a sufficient outlet in detective stories, where I alternatively identify myself with the murderer and the huntsman-detective, but I know there are those to whom this vicarious outlet is too mild, and for them something stronger should be provided.

I do not think that ordinary human beings can be happy without competition, for competition has been, ever since the origin of Man, the spur to most serious activities. We should not, therefore, attempt to abolish competition, but only see to it that it takes forms which are not too injurious. Primitive competition was a conflict as to which should murder the other man and his wife and children; modern competition in the shape of war still takes this form. But in sport, in literary and artistic rivalry, and in constitutional politics it takes forms which do very little harm and yet offer a fairly adequate outlet for our combative instincts. What is wrong in this respect is not that such forms of competition are bad, but that they form too small a part of the lives of ordinary men and women.

Apart from war, modern civilisation has aimed increasingly at security, but I am not at all sure that the elimination of all danger makes for happiness. I should like at this point to quote a passage from Sir Arthur Keith's *New Theory of Human Evolution*:

> Those who have visited the peoples living under a reign of "wild justice" bring back accounts of happiness among natives living under such conditions. Freya Stark, for example, reported thus of South Arabia: "When I came to travel in that part of the country where security is non-existent, I found a people, though full of lament over their life of perpetual blackmail and robbery,

yet just as cheerful and as full of the ordinary joy of living as anywhere on earth." Dr H. K. Fry had a similar experience among the aborigines of Australia. "A native in his wild state," he reports, "lives in constant danger, hostile spirits are about him constantly. Yet he is light-hearted and cheerful . . . indulgent to his children and kind to his aged parents." My third illustration is taken from the Crow Indians of America, who have been living under the eye of Dr R. Lowrie for many years. They are now living in the security of a reserve. "Ask a Crow," reports Dr Lowrie, "whether he would have security as now, or danger as of old, and his answer is – 'danger as of old . . . there was glory in it.' " I am assuming that the wild conditions of life I have been describing were those amid which mankind lived through the whole of the primal period of its evolution. It was amid such conditions that man's nature and character were fashioned, one of the conditions being the practice of blood-revenge.

Such effects of human psychology account for some things which, for me at least, were surprising when in 1914 I first became aware of them. Many people are happier during a war than they are in peace time, provided the direct suffering entailed by the fighting does not fall too heavily upon them personally. A quiet life may well be a boring life. The unadventurous existence of a well-behaved citizen, engaged in earning a moderate living in a humble capacity, leaves completely unsatisfied all that part of his nature which, if he had lived 400,000 years ago, would have found ample scope in the search for food, in cutting off the heads of enemies, and in escaping the attention of tigers. When war comes the bank clerk may escape and become a commando, and then at last he feels that he is living as nature intended him to live. But, unfortunately, science has put into our hands such enormously powerful means of satisfying our destructive instincts, that to allow them free play no longer serves any evolutionary purpose, as it did while men were divided into petty tribes. The problem of making peace with our anarchic impulses is one which has been too little studied, but one which becomes more and more imperative as scientific technique advances. From the purely biological point of view it is unfortunate that the destructive side of technique has advanced so very much more rapidly than the creative side. In one moment a man may kill 500,000 people, but he cannot have children any quicker than in the days of our savage ancestors. If a man could have 500,000 children as quickly as by an atomic bomb he can destroy 500,000 enemies, we might, at the cost of enormous suffering, leave the biological problem to the struggle for existence and the survival of the fittest. But in the modern world the old mechanism of evolution can no longer be relied upon.

The problem of the social reformer, therefore, is not *merely* to seek means of security, for if these means when found provide no deep satisfaction the security will be thrown away for the glory of adventure. The problem is rather to combine that degree of security which is essential to the species, with forms of adventure and danger and contest which are compatible with the civilised way of life. And in attempting to solve this problem we must remember always that, although our manner of life and our institutions and our knowledge have undergone profound changes, our instincts for both good and evil remain very much what they were when our ancestors' brains first grew to their present size. I do not think the reconciliation of primitive impulses with the civilised way of life is impossible, and the studies of anthropologists have shown the very wide adaptability of human nature to different culture patterns. But I do not think it can be achieved by complete exclusion of any basic impulse. A life without adventure is likely to be unsatisfying, but a life in which adventure is allowed to take whatever form it will is sure to be short.

I think perhaps the essence of the matter was given by the Red

Indian whom I quoted a moment ago, who regretted the old life because 'there was glory in it.' Every energetic person wants something that can count as 'glory.' There are those who get it – film stars, famous athletes, military commanders, and even some few politicians, but they are a small minority, and the rest are left to day-dreams – day-dreams of the cinema, day-dreams of wild west adventure stories, purely private day-dreams of imaginary power. I am not one of those who think day-dreams wholly evil; they are an essential part of the life of imagination. But when throughout a long life there is no means of relating them to reality they easily become unwholesesome and even dangerous to sanity. Perhaps it may still be possible, even in our mechanical world, to find some real outlet for the impulses which are now confined to the realm of phantasy. In the interests of stability it is much to be hoped that this may be possible, for, if it is not, destructive philosophies will from time to time sweep away the best of human achievements. If this is to be prevented, the savage in each one of us must find some outlet not incompatible with civilised life and the happiness of his equally savage neighbour.

Lecture 2

SOCIAL COHESION
AND GOVERNMENT

The original mechanism of social cohesion, as it is still to be found among the most primitive races, was one which operated through individual psychology without the need of anything that could be called government. There were, no doubt, tribal customs which all had to obey, but one must suppose that there was no impulse to disobedience of these customs and no need of magistrates or policemen to enforce them. In Old Stone Age times, so far as authority was concerned, the tribe seems to have lived in a state which we should now describe as anarchy. But it differed from what anarchy would be in a modern community owing to the fact that social impulses sufficiently controlled the acts of individuals. Men of the New Stone Age were already quite different; they had government, authorities capable of exacting obedience, and large-scale enforced co-operation. This is evident from their works; the primitive type of small-tribe cohesion could not have produced Stonehenge, still less the Pyramids. The enlargement of the social unit must have been mainly the result of war. If two tribes had a war of extermination, the victorious tribe by the acquisition of new territory would be able to increase its numbers. There would also in war be an obvious advantage in an alliance of two or more tribes. If the danger producing the alliance persisted, the alliance would, in time, become an amalgamation. When a unit became too large for all its members to know each other, there would come to be a need of some mechanism for arriving at collective decisions, and this mechanism would inevitably develop by stages into something that a modern man could recognise as government. As soon as there is government some men have more power than others, and the power that they have depends, broadly speaking, upon the size of the unit that they govern. Love of power, therefore, will cause the governors to desire conquest. This motive is very much reinforced when the vanquished are made into slaves instead of being exterminated. In this way, at a very early age, communities arose in which, although primitive impulses towards social co-operation still existed, they were immensely reinforced by the power of the government to punish those who disobeyed it. In the earliest fully historical community, that of ancient Egypt, we find a king whose powers over a large territory were absolute, except for some limitation by the priesthood, and we find a large servile population whom the king could at his will, employ upon State enterprises such as the Pyramids. In such a community only a minority at the top of the social scale – the king, the aristocracy, and the priests – needed any psychological mechanism towards social cohesion; all the rest merely obeyed. No doubt large parts of the population were unhappy; one can get a picture of their condition from the first chapters of Exodus. But as a rule, so long as external enemies were not to be feared, this condition of widespread suffering did not prevent the prosperity of the State, and it left unimpaired the enjoyment of life by the holders of power. This state of affairs must have existed for long ages throughout what we now call the

Middle East. It depended for its stability upon religion and the divinity of the king. Disobedience was impiety, and rebellion was liable to call down the anger of the gods. So long as the upper social layers genuinely believed this, the rest would be merely disciplined as we now discipline domestic animals.

It is a curious fact that military conquest very often produced in the conquered a genuine loyalty towards their masters. This happened in time with most of the Roman conquests. In the fifth century, when Rome could no longer *compel* obedience, Gaul remained completely loyal to the Empire. All the states of antiquity owed their existence to military power, but most of them were able, if they lasted long enough, to generate a sense of cohesion in the whole in spite of the violent resistance of many parts at the time of their incorporation. The same thing happened again with the growth of modern States during the Middle Ages. England, France, and Spain all acquired unity as a result of military victory by a ruler of some part of what became a single nation.

In antiquity all large States, except Egypt, suffered from a lack of stability of which the causes were largely technical. When nothing could move faster than a horse it was difficult for the central government to keep a firm hold upon outlying satraps or pro-consuls, who were apt to rebel, sometimes succeeding in conquering the whole Empire and at other times making themselves independent sovereigns of a part of it. Alexander, Atilla, and Jenghiz Khan had vast empires which broke up at their death, and in which unity had depended entirely upon the prestige of a great conqueror. These various empires had no psychological unity, but only the unity of force. Rome did better, because Graeco-Roman civilisation was something which educated individuals valued and which was sharply contrasted with the barbarism of tribes beyond the frontier. Until the invention of modern techniques it was scarcely possible to hold a large empire together unless the upper sections of society throughout its length and breadth had some common sentiment by which they were united. And the ways of generating such a common sentiment were much less understood than they are now. The psychological basis of social cohesion, therefore, was still important, although needed only among a governing minority. In ancient communities the chief advantage of great size, namely the possibility of large armies, was balanced by the disadvantage that it took a long time to move an army from one part of the empire to another, and also that the civil government had not discovered ways of preventing military insurrection. To some degree these conditions lasted on into modern times. It was largely lack of mobility that caused England, Spain and Portugal to lose their possessions in the Western Hemisphere. But since the coming of steam and the telegraph it has become much easier than it was before to hold a large territory, and since the coming of universal education it has become easier to instill more or less artificial loyalty throughout a large population.

Modern technique has not only facilitated the psychology of cohesion in large groups; it has also made large groups imperative both from an economic and from a military point of view. The advantages of mass production are a trite theme, upon which I do not propose to enlarge. As everybody knows, they have been urged as a reason for closer unity among the nations of Western Europe. The Nile from the earliest times has promoted the cohesion of the whole of Egypt, since a government controlling only the upper Nile could destroy the fertility of lower Egypt. Here no advanced technique was involved, but the Tennessee Valley Authority and the proposed St Lawrence Water Way are scientific extensions of the same cohesive effect of rivers. Central power stations, distributing electricity over wide areas, have become increasingly important, and are much more profitable when the area is large than when it is small. If it becomes practicable (as is not unlikely) to use atomic power on a large scale, this will enormously augment the profitable area of distribution.

All of these modern developments increase the control over the lives of individuals possessed by those who govern large organisations, and at the same time make a few large organisations much more productive than a number of smaller ones. Short of the whole planet there is no visible limit to the advantages of size, both in economic and in political organisations.

I come now to another survey of roughly the same governmental developments from a different point of view. Governmental control over the lives of members of the community has differed throughout history, not only in the size of the governmental area, but in the intensity of its interference with individual life. What may be called civilisation begins with empires of a well-defined type, of which Egypt, Babylon, and Nineveh are the most notable; the Aztec and Inca empires were essentially of the same type. In such empires the upper caste had at first a considerable measure of personal initiative, but the large slave population acquired in foreign conquest had none. The priesthood were able to interfere in daily life to a very great degree. Except where religion was involved, the King had absolute power, and could compel his subjects to fight in his wars. The divinity of the King and the reverence for the priesthood produced a stable society – in the case of Egypt, the most stable of which we have any knowledge. This stability was bought at the expense of rigidity. And these ancient empires became stereotyped to a point at which they could no longer resist foreign aggression; they were absorbed by Persia, and Persia in the end was defeated by the Greeks.

The Greeks perfected a new type of civilisation that had been inaugurated by the Phoenicians: that of the City State based on commerce and sea power. Greek cities differed greatly as regards the degree of individual liberty permitted to citizens; in most of them there was a great deal, but in Sparta an absolute minimum. Most of them tended, however, to fall under the sway of tyrants, and throughout considerable periods had a regime of despotism tempered by revolution. In a City State revolution was easy. Malcontents had only to traverse a few miles to get beyond the territory of the government against which they wished to rebel, and there were always hostile City States ready to help them. Throughout the great age of Greece there was a degree of anarchy which to a modern mind would seem intolerable. But the citizens of a Greek city, even those who were in rebellion against the actual government, had retained a psychology of primitive loyalty; they loved their own city with a devotion which was often unwise but almost always passionate. The greatness of the Greeks in individual achievement was, I think, intimately bound up with their political incompetence, for the strength of individual passion was the source both of individual achievement and of the failure to secure Greek unity. And so Greece fell under the domination, first of Macedonia, and then of Rome.

The Roman Empire, while it was expanding, left a very considerable degree of individual and local autonomy in the Provinces, but after Augustus government gradually acquired a greater and greater degree of control, and in the end, chiefly through the severity of taxation, caused the whole system to break down over the greater part of what had been the Roman Empire. In what remained, however, there was no relaxation of control. It was objection to this minute control, more than any other cause, that made Justinian's re-conquest of Italy and Africa so transitory. For those who had first welcomed his legions as deliverers from the Goths and Vandals changed their minds when the legions were followed by an army of tax gatherers.

Rome's attempt to unify the civilised world came to grief largely because, perhaps through being both remote and alien, it failed to bring any measure of instinctive happiness even to prosperous citizens. In its last centuries there was universal pessimism and lack of vigour. Men felt that life here on earth had little to offer, and this feeling helped Christianity to centre men's thoughts on the world to come.

With the eclipse of Rome the West underwent a very complete transformation. Commerce almost ceased, the great Roman roads fell into disrepair, petty kings constantly went to war with each other, and governed small territories as best they could, while they had to meet the anarchy of a turbulent Teutonic aristocracy and the sullen dislike of the old Romanised population. Slavery on a large scale almost disappeared throughout Western Christendom, but was replaced by serfdom. In place of being supported by the vast fleets that brought grain from Africa to Rome, small communities with few and rare external contacts lived as best they could on the produce of their own land. Life was hard and rough, but it had no longer the quality of listlessness and hopelessness that it had had in the last days of Rome. Throughout the Dark Ages and Middle Ages lawlessness was rampant, with the result that all thoughtful men worshipped law. Gradually the vigour which lawlessness had permitted restored a measure of order and enabled a series of great men to build up a new civilisation.

From the fifteenth century to the present time the power of the State as against the individual has been continually increasing, at first mainly as a result of the invention of gunpowder. Just as, in the earlier days of anarchy, the most thoughtful men worshipped law, so during the period of increasing State power there was a growing tendency to worship liberty. The eighteenth and nineteenth centuries had a remarkable degree of success in increasing State power to what was necessary for the preservation of order, and leaving in spite of it a great measure of freedom to those citizens who did not belong to the lowest social grades. The impulse towards liberty, however, seems now to have lost much of its force among reformers; it has been replaced by the love of equality, which has been largely stimulated by the rise to affluence and power of new industrial magnates without any traditional claim to superiority. And the exigencies of total war have persuaded almost everybody that a

much tighter social system is necessary than that which con-
tented our grandfathers.

There is over a large part of the earth's surface something
not unlike a reversion to the ancient Egyptian system of divine
kingship, controlled by a new priestly caste. Although this tendency has not gone so far in the West as it has in the East, it has,
nevertheless, gone to lengths which would have astonished the
eighteenth and nineteenth centuries both in England and in
America. Individual initiative is hemmed in either by the State
or by powerful corporations, and there is a great danger lest this
should produce, as in ancient Rome, a kind of listlessness and
fatalism that is disastrous to vigorous life. I am constantly receiv-
ing letters saying: 'I see that the world is in a bad state, but what
can one humble person do? Life and property are at the mercy
of a few individuals who have the decision as to peace or war.
Economic activities on any large scale are determined by those
who govern either the State or the large corporations. Even
where there is nominally democracy, the part which one citizen
can obtain in controlling policy is usually infinitesimal. Is it not
perhaps better in such circumstances to forget public affairs and
get as much enjoyment by the way as the times permit?' I find
such letters very difficult to answer, and I am sure that the state
of mind which leads to their being written is very inimical to a
healthy social life. As a result of mere size, government becomes
increasingly remote from the governed and tends, even in a
democracy, to have an independent life of its own. I do not
profess to know how to cure this evil completely, but I think it
is important to recognise its existence and to search for ways
of diminishing its magnitude.

The instinctive mechanism of social cohesion, namely loyalty
to a small tribe whose members are all known to each other, is
something very remote indeed from the kind of loyalty to a
large State which has replaced it in the modern world, and even
what remains of the more primitive kind of loyalty is likely to

disappear in the new organisation of the world that present dangers call for. An Englishman or a Scotsman can feel an instinctive loyalty to Britain: he may know what Shakespeare has to say about it; he knows that it is an island with boundaries that are wholly natural; he is aware of English history, in so far, at least, as it is glorious, and he knows that people on the Continent speak foreign languages. But if loyalty to Britain is to be replaced by loyalty to Western Union, there will need to be a consciousness of Western culture as something with a unity transcending national boundaries; for apart from this there is only one pyschological motive which is adequate for the purpose, and that is the motive of fear of external enemies. But fear is a negative motive, and one which ceases to be operative in the moment of victory. When it is compared with the love of a Greek for his native city it is obvious how very much smaller is the hold which loyalty based merely on fear has on the instincts and passions of ordinary men and women in the absence of immediate and pressing dangers.

Government, from the earliest times at which it existed, has had two functions, one negative and one positive. Its negative function has been to prevent private violence, to protect life and property, to enact criminal law and secure its enforcement. But in addition to this it has had a positive purpose, namely, to facilitate the realisation of desires deemed to be common to the great majority of citizens. The positive functions of government at most times have been mainly confined to war: if an enemy could be conquered and his territory acquired, everybody in the victorious nation profited in a greater or less degree. But now the positive functions of government are enormously enlarged. There is first of all education, consisting not only of the acquisition of scholastic attainments, but also of the instilling of certain loyalties and certain beliefs. These are those which the State considers desirable, and, in a lesser degree, in some cases, those demanded by some religious body. Then there are vast industrial enterprises. Even in the United States, which attempts to limit the economic activities of the State to the utmost possible degree, governmental control over such enterprises is rapidly increasing. And as regards industrial enterprises there is little difference, from the psychological point of view, between those conducted by the State and those conducted by large private corporations. In either case there is a government which in fact, if not in intention, is remote from those whom it controls. It is only the members of the government, whether of a State or of a large corporation, who can retain the sense of individual initiative, and there is inevitably a tendency for governments to regard those who work for them more or less as they regard their machines, that is to say, merely as necessary means. The desirability of smooth co-operation constantly tends to increase the size of units, and therefore to diminish the number of those who still possess the power of initiative. Worst of all, from our present point of view, is a system which exists over wide fields in Britain, where those who have nominal initiative are perpetually controlled by a Civil Service which has only a veto and no duty of inauguration, and thus acquires a negative psychology perpetually prone to prohibitions. Under such a system the energetic are reduced to despair; those who might have become energetic in a more hopeful environment tend to be listless and frivolous; and it is not likely that the positive functions of the State will be performed with vigour and competence. It is probable that economic entomology could bring in enormously greater profits than it does at present, but this would require the sanctioning of the salaries of a considerable number of entomologists, and at present the government is of the opinion that a policy so enterprising as employing entomologists should only be applied with timidity. This, needless to say, is the opinion of men who have acquired the habit that one sees in unwise parents of always saying 'don't do that,' without stopping to consider whether 'that' does any harm. Such evils are very hard to avoid where there is remote control, and there is likely to be much remote control in any organisation which is very large.

I shall consider in a later lecture what can be done to mitigate these evils without losing the indubitable advantages of large scale organisation. It may be that the present tendencies towards centralisation are too strong to be resisted until they have led to disaster, and that, as happened in the fifth century, the whole system must break down, with all the inevitable results of anarchy and poverty, before human beings can again acquire that degree of personal freedom without which life loses its savour. I hope that this is not the case, but it certainly will be the case unless the danger is realised and unless vigorous measures are taken to combat it.

In this brief sketch of the changes in regard to social cohesion that have occurred in historical times, we may observe a two-fold movement.

On the one hand, there is a periodic development, from a loose and primitive type of organisation to a gradually more orderly government, embracing a wider area, and regulating a greater part of the lives of individuals. At a certain point in this development, when there has recently been a great increase in wealth and security, but the vigour and enterprise of wilder ages has not yet decayed, there are apt to be great achievements in the way of advancing civilisation. But when the new civilisation becomes stereotyped, when government has had time to consolidate its power, when custom, tradition, and law have established rules sufficiently minute to choke enterprise, the society concerned enters upon a stagnant phase. Men praise the exploits of their ancestors, but can no longer equal them; art becomes conventional, and science is stifled by respect for authority.

This type of development followed by ossification is to be found in China and India, in Mesopotamia and Egypt, and in the Graeco-Roman world. The end comes usually through foreign conquest: there are old maxims for fighting old enemies, but when an enemy of a new type arises the elderly community has not the adaptability to adopt the new maxims that can alone bring safety. If, as often happens, the conquerors are less civilised than the conquered, they have probably not the skill for the government of a large empire, or for the preservation of commerce over a wide area. The result is a diminution of population, of the size of governmental units, and of the intensity of governmental control. Gradually, in the new more or less anarchic conditions, vigour returns, and a new cycle begins.

But in addition to this periodic movement there is another. At the apex of each cycle, the area governed by one State is larger than at any former time, and the degree of control exercised by authority over the individual is more intense than in any previous culmination. The Roman Empire was larger than the Babylonian and Egyptian empires, and the empires of the present day are larger than that of Rome. There has never in past history been any large State that controlled its citizens as completely as they are controlled in the Soviet Republic, or even in the countries of Western Europe.

Since the earth is of finite size, this tendency, if unchecked, must end in the creation of a single world State. But as there will then be no external enemy to promote cohesion through fear, the old psychological mechanisms will no longer be adequate. There will be no scope for patriotism in the affairs of the world government; the driving force will have to be found in self-interest and benevolence, without the potent incentives of hate and fear. Can such a society persist? And if it persists, can it be capable of progress? These are difficult questions. Some considerations that must be borne in mind if they are to be answered will be brought forward in subsequent lectures.

I have spoken of a two-fold movement in past history, but I do not consider that there is anything either certain or inevitable about such laws of historical development as we can discover. New knowledge may make the course of events completely different from what it would otherwise have been; this was, for instance, a result of the discovery of America. New institutions also may have effects that could not have been foreseen; I do not see how any Roman at the time of Julius Caesar could have predicted anything at all like the Catholic Church. And no one in the nineteenth century, not even Marx, foresaw the Soviet Union. For such reasons, all prophecies as to the future of mankind should be treated only as hypotheses which may deserve consideration.

I think that, while all definite prophecy is rash, there are certain undesirable possibilities which it is wise to bear in mind. On the one hand, prolonged and destructive war may cause a breakdown of industry in all civilised States, leading to a condition of small-scale anarchy such as prevailed in Western Europe after the fall of Rome. This would involve an immense diminution of the population, and, for a time at least, a cessation of many of the activities that we consider characteristic of a civilised way of life. But it would seem reasonable to hope that, as happened in the Middle Ages, a sufficient minimum of social cohesion would in time be restored, and the lost ground would gradually be recovered.

There is, however, another danger, perhaps more likely to be realised. Modern techniques have made possible a new intensity of governmental control, and this possibility has been exploited very fully in totalitarian States. It may be that under the stress of war, or the fear of war, or as a result of totalitarian conquest, the parts of the world where some degree of individual liberty survives may grow fewer, and even in them liberty may come to be more and more restricted. There is not much reason to suppose that the resulting system would be unstable, but it would almost certainly be static and unprogressive. And it would bring with it a recrudescence of ancient evils: slavery, bigotry, intolerance, and abject misery for the majority of mankind. This is, to my mind, a misfortune against which it is of the utmost importance to be on our guard. For this reason, emphasis upon the value of the individual is even more necessary now than at any former time.

There is another fallacy which it is important to avoid. I think it is true, as I have been arguing, that what is congenital in human nature has probably changed little during hundreds of thousands of years, but what is congenital is only a small part of the mental structure of a modern human being. From what I have been saying I should not wish anyone to draw the inference that in a world without war there would necessarily be a sense of instinctive frustration. Sweden has never been at war since 1814, that is to say, for a period of four generations, but I do not think anybody could maintain that the Swedes have suffered in their instinctive life as a result of this immunity. If mankind succeeds in abolishing war, it should not be difficult to find other outlets for the love of adventure and risk. The old outlets, which at one time served a biological purpose, do so no longer, and therefore new outlets are necessary. But there is nothing in human nature that compels us to acquiesce in continued savagery. Our less orderly impulses are dangerous only when they are denied or misunderstood. When this mistake is avoided, the problem of fitting them into a good social system can be solved by the help of intelligence and goodwill.

Lecture 3

THE ROLE OF INDIVIDUALITY

In this lecture I propose to consider the importance, for both good and evil, of impulses and desires that belong to some members of a community but not to all. In a very primitive community such impulses and desires play very little part. Hunting and war are activities in which one man may be more successful than another, but in which all share a common purpose. So long as a man's spontaneous activities are such as all the tribe approves of and shares in, his initiative is very little curbed by others within the tribe, and even his most spontaneous actions conform to the recognised pattern of behaviour. But as men grow more civilised there comes to be an increasing difference between one man's activities and another's, and a community needs, if it is to prosper, a certain number of individuals who do not wholly conform to the general type. Practically all progress, artistic, moral, and intellectual, has depended upon such individuals, who have been a decisive factor in the transition from barbarism to civilisation. If a community is to make progress, it needs exceptional individuals whose activities, though useful, are not of a sort that ought to be general. There is always a tendency in highly organised society for the activities of such individuals to be unduly hampered, but on the other hand, if the community exercises no control, the same kind of individual initiative which may produce a valuable innovator may also produce a criminal. The problem, like all those with which we are concerned, is one of balance; too little liberty brings stagnation, and too much brings chaos.

There are many ways in which an individual may differ from most of the other members of his herd. He may be exceptionally anarchic or criminal; he may have rare artistic talent; he may have what comes in time to be recognised as a new wisdom in matters of religion and morals, and he may have exceptional intellectual powers. It would seem that from a very early period in human history there must have been some differentiation of function. The pictures in the caves in the Pyrenees which were made by Paleolithic men have a very high degree of artistic merit, and one can hardly suppose that all the men of that time were capable of such admirable work. It seems far more probable that those who were found to have artistic talent were sometimes allowed to stay at home making pictures while the rest of the tribe hunted. The chief and the priest must have begun from a very early time to be chosen for real or supposed peculiar excellences: medicine men could work magic, and the tribal spirit was in some sense incarnate in the chief. But from the earliest time there has been a tendency for every activity of this kind to become institutionalised. The chieftain became hereditary, the medicine men became a separate caste, and recognised bards became the prototypes of our Poets Laureate. It has always been difficult for communities to recognise what is necessary for individuals who are going to make the kind of exceptional contribution that I have in mind, namely, elements of wildness, of separateness from the herd, of domination by rare impulses of which the utility was not always obvious to everybody.

In this lecture I wish to consider both in history and in the present day the relation of the exceptional man to the community, and the conditions that make it easy for his unusual merits to be socially fruitful. I shall consider this problem first in art, then in religion and morals, and, finally, in science.

The artist in our day does not play nearly so vital a part in public life as he has done in many former ages. There is a tendency in our days to despise a Court poet, and to think that a poet should be a solitary being proclaiming something that Philistines do not wish to hear. Historically the matter was far otherwise; Homer, Virgil, and Shakespeare were Court Poets, they sang the glories of their tribe and its noble traditions. (Of Shakespeare, I must confess, this is only partially true, but it certainly applies to his historical plays.) Welsh bards kept alive the glories of King Arthur, and these glories came to be celebrated by English and French writers; King Henry II encouraged them for imperialistic reasons. The glories of the Parthenon and of the medieval cathedrals were intimately bound up with public objects. Music, though it would play its part in courtship, existed primarily to promote courage in battle – a purpose to which, according to Plato, it ought to be confined by law. But of these ancient glories of the artist little remains in the modern world except the piper to a Highland regiment. We still honour the artist, but we isolate him; we think of art as something separate, not as an integral part of the life of the community. The architect alone, because his art serves a utilitarian purpose, retains something of the ancient status of the artist.

The decay of art in our time is not only due to the fact that the social function of the artist is not as important as in former days; it is due also to the fact that spontaneous delight is no longer felt as something which it is important to be able to enjoy. Among comparatively unsophisticated populations folk dances and popular music still flourish, and something of the poet exists in very many men. But as men grow more industrialised and regimented, the kind of delight that is common in children becomes impossible to adults, because they are always thinking of the next thing, and cannot let themselves be absorbed in the moment. This habit of thinking of the 'next thing' is more fatal to any kind of aesthetic excellence than any other habit of mind that can be imagined, and if art, in any important sense, is to survive, it will not be by the foundation of solemn academies, but by recapturing the capacity for wholehearted joys and sorrows which prudence and foresight have all but destroyed.

The men conventionally recognised as the greatest of mankind have been innovators in religion and morals. In spite of the reverence given to them by subsequent ages, most of them during their lifetime were in a greater or less degree in conflict with their own communities. Moral progress has consisted, in the main, of protest against cruel customs, and of attempts to enlarge the bounds of human sympathy. Human sacrifice among the Greeks died out at the beginning of the fully historical epoch. The Stoics taught that there should be sympathy not only for free Greeks but for barbarians and slaves, and, indeed, for all mankind. Buddhism and Christianity spread a similar doctrine far and wide. Religion, which had originally been part of the apparatus of tribal cohesion, promoting conflict without just as much as co-operation within, took on a more universal character, and endeavoured to transcend the narrow limits which primitive morality had set. It is no wonder if the religious innovators were execrated in their own day, for they sought to rob men of the joy of battle and the fierce delights of revenge. Primitive ferocity, which had seemed a virtue, was now said to be a sin, and a deep duality was introduced between morality and the life of impulse – or rather between the morality taught by those in whom the impulse of humanity was strong, and the traditional morality that was preferred by those who had no sympathies outside their own herd.

Religious and moral innovators have had an immense effect

upon human life, not always, it must be confessed, the effect that they intended, but nevertheless on the whole profoundly beneficial. It is true that in the present century we have seen in important parts of the world a loss of moral values which we had thought fairly secure, but we may hope that this retrogression will not last. We owe it to the moral innovators who first attempted to make morality a universal and not merely a tribal matter, that there has come to be a disapproval of slavery, a feeling of duty towards prisoners of war, a limitation of the powers of husbands and fathers, and a recognition, however imperfect, that subject races ought not to be merely exploited for the benefit of their conquerors. All these moral gains, it must be admitted, have been jeopardised by a recrudescence of ancient ferocity, but I do not think that in the end the moral advance which they have represented will be lost to mankind.

The prophets and sages who inaugurated this moral advance, although for the most part they were not honoured in their own day, were, nevertheless, not prevented from doing their work. In a modern totalitarian State matters are worse than they were in the time of Socrates, or in the time of the Gospels. In a totalitarian State an innovator whose ideas are disliked by the government is not merely put to death, which is a matter to which a brave man may remain indifferent, but is totally prevented from causing his doctrine to be known. Innovations in such a community can come only from the government, and the government now, as in the past, is not likely to approve of anything contrary to its own immediate interests. In a totalitarian State such events as the rise of Buddhism or Christianity are scarcely possible, and not even by the greatest heroism can a moral reformer acquire an influence whatever. This is a new fact in human history, brought about by the much increased control over individuals which the modern technique of government has made possible. It is a very grave fact, and one which shows how fatal a totalitarian regime must be to every kind of moral progress.

In our own day an individual of exceptional powers can hardly hope to have so great a career or so great a social influence as in former times, if he devotes himself to art or to religious and moral reform. There are, however, still four careers which are open to him; he may become a great political leader, like Lenin; he may acquire vast industrial power, like Rockefeller; he may transform the world by scientific discoveries, as is being done by the atomic physicists; or, finally, if he has not the necessary capacities for any of these careers, or if opportunity is lacking, his energy in default of other outlet may drive him into a life of crime. Criminals, in the legal sense, seldom have much influence upon the course of history, and therefore a man of overweening ambition will choose some other career if it is open to him.

The rise of men of science to great eminence in the State is a modern phenomenon. Scientists, like other innovators, had to fight for recognition: some were banished; some were burnt; some were kept in dungeons; others merely had their books burnt. But gradually it came to be realised that they could put power into the hands of the State. The French revolutionaries, after mistakenly guillotining Lavoisier, employed his surviving colleagues in the manufacture of explosives. In modern war the scientists are recognised by all civilised governments as the most useful citizens, provided they can be tamed and induced to place their services at the disposal of a single government rather than of mankind.

For both good and evil almost everything that distinguishes our age from its predecessors is due to science. In daily life we have electric light, and the radio, and the cinema. In industry we employ machinery and power which we owe to science. Because of the increased productivity of labour we are able to devote a far greater proportion of our energies to wars and preparations for wars than was formerly possible, and we are able to keep the young in school very much longer than we formerly could. Owing to science we are able to disseminate information and misinformation through the Press and the radio to practically everybody. Owing to science we can make it enormously more difficult than it used to be for people whom the government dislikes to escape. The whole of our daily life and our social organisation is what it is because of science. The whole of this vast development is supported nowadays by the State, but it grew up originally in opposition to the State, and where, as in Russia, the State has reverted to an earlier pattern, the old opposition would again appear if the State were not omnipotent to a degree undreamt of by the tyrants of former ages.

The opposition to science in the past was by no means surprising. Men of science affirmed things that were contrary to what everybody had believed; they upset preconceived ideas and were thought to be destitute of reverence. Anaxagoras taught that the sun was a red-hot stone and that the moon was made of earth. For this impiety he was banished from Athens, for was it not well known that the sun was a god and the moon a goddess? It was only the power over natural forces conferred by science that led bit by bit to a toleration of scientists, and even this was a very slow process, because their powers were at first attributed to magic.

It would not be surprising if, in the present day, a powerful anti-scientific movement were to arise as a result of the dangers to human life that are resulting from atom bombs and may result from bacteriological warfare. But whatever people may feel about these horrors, they dare not turn against the men of science so long as war is at all probable, because if one side were equipped with scientists and the other not, the scientific side would almost certainly win.

Science, in so far as it consists of knowledge, must be regarded as having value, but in so far as it consists of technique the question whether it is to be praised or blamed depends upon the use that is made of the technique. In itself it is neutral, neither good nor bad, and any ultimate views that we may have about what gives value to this or that must come from some other source than science.

The men of science, in spite of their profound influence upon modern life, are in some ways less powerful than the politicians. Politicians in our day are far more influential than they were at any former period in human history. Their relation to the men of science is like that of a magician in the Arabian Nights to a djinn who obeys his orders. The djinn does astounding things which the magician, without his help, could not do, but he does them only because he is told to do them, not because of any impulse in himself. So it is with the atomic scientists in our day; some government captures them in their homes or on the high seas, and they are set to work, according to the luck of their capture, to slave for the one side or for the other. The politician, when he is successful, is subject to no such coercion. The most astounding career of our times was that of Lenin. After his brother had been put to death by the Czarist Government, he spent years in poverty and exile, and then rose within a few months to command of one of the greatest of States. And this command was not like that of Xerxes or Caesar, merely the power to enjoy luxury and adulation, which but for him some other man would have been enjoying. It was the power to mould a vast country according to a pattern conceived in his own mind, to alter the life of every worker, every peasant, and every middle-class person; to introduce a totally new kind of organisation, and to become throughout the world the symbol of a new order, admired by some, execrated by many, but ignored by none. No megalomaniac's dream could have been more terrific. Napoleon had asserted that you can do everything with bayonets except sit upon them; Lenin disproved the exception.

The great men who stand out in history have been partly benefactors of mankind and partly quite the reverse. Some, like the great religious and moral innovators, have done what lay in their power to make men less cruel towards each other, and less limited in their sympathies; some, like the men of science, have given us a knowledge and understanding of natural processes which, however it may be misused, must be regarded as in itself a splendid thing. Some, like the great poets and composers and painters, have put into the world beauties and splendours which, in moments of discouragement, do much to make the spectacle of human destiny endurable. But others, equally able, equally effective in their way, have done quite the opposite. I cannot think of anything that mankind has gained by the existence of Jenghis Khan. I do not know what good came of Robespierre, and, for my part, I see no reason to be grateful to Lenin. But all these men, good and bad alike, had a quality which I should not wish to see disappear from the world – a quality of energy and personal initiative, of independence of mind, and of imaginative vision. A man who possesses these qualities is capable of doing much good, or of doing great harm, and if mankind is not to sink into dullness such exceptional men must find scope, though one could wish that the scope they find should be for the benefit of mankind. There may be less difference than is sometimes thought between the temperament of a great criminal and a great statesman. It may be that Captain Kidd and Alexander the Great, if a magician had interchanged them at birth, would have each fulfilled the career which, in fact, was fulfilled by the other. The same thing may be said of some artists; the memoirs of Benvenuto Cellini do not give a picture of a man with that respect for law which every right-minded citizen ought to have. In the modern world, and still more, so far as can be guessed, in the world of the near future, important achievement is and will be almost impossible to an individual if he cannot dominate some vast organisation. If he can make himself head of a State like Lenin, or monopolist of a great industry like Rockefeller, or a controller of credit like the elder Pierpont Morgan, he can produce enormous effects in the world. And so he can if, being a man of science, he persuades some government that his work may be useful in war. But the man who works without the help of an organisation, like a Hebrew prophet, a poet, or a solitary philosopher such as Spinoza, can no longer hope for the kind of importance which such men had in former days. The change applies to the scientist as well as to other men. The scientists of the past did their work very largely as individuals, but the scientist of our day needs enormously expensive equipment and a laboratory with many assistants. All this he can obtain through the favour of the government, or, in America, of very rich men. He is thus no longer an independent worker, but essentially part and parcel of some large organisation. This change is very fortunate, for the things which a great man could do in solitude were apt to be more beneficial than those which he can only do with the help of the powers that be. A man who wishes to influence human affairs finds it difficult to be successful, except as a slave or a tyrant: as a politician he may make himself the head of a State, or as a scientist he may sell his labour to the government, but in that case he must serve its purposes and not his own.

And this applies not only to men of rare and exceptional greatness, but to a wide range of talent. In the ages in which there were great poets, there were also large numbers of little poets, and when there were great painters there were large numbers of little painters. The great German composers arose in a milieu where music was valued, and where numbers of lesser men found opportunities. In those days poetry, painting, and music were a vital part of the daily life of ordinary men, as only sport is now. The great prophets were men who stood out from a host of minor prophets. The inferiority of our age in such respects is an inevitable result of the fact that society is centralised and organised to such a degree that individual initiative is reduced to a minimum. Where art has flourished in the past it has flourished as a rule amongst small communities which had rivals among their neighbours, such as the Greek City States, the little Principalities of the Italian Renaissance, and the petty Courts of German eighteenth-century rulers. Each of these rulers had to have his musician, and once in a way he was Johann Sebastian Bach, but even if he was not he was still free to do his best. There is something about local rivalry that is essential in such matters. It played its part even in the building of the cathedrals, because each bishop wished to have a finer cathedral than the neighbouring bishop. It would be a good thing if cities could develop an artistic pride leading them to mutual rivalry, and if each had its own school of music and painting, not without a vigorous contempt for the school of the next city. But such local patriotisms do not readily flourish in a world of empires and free mobility. A Manchester man does not readily feel towards a man from Sheffield as an Athenian felt towards a Corinthian, or a Florentine towards a Venetian. But in spite of the difficulties, I think that this problem of giving importance to localities will have to be tackled if human life is not to become increasingly drab and monotonous.

The savage, in spite of his membership of a small community, lived a life in which his initiative was not too much hampered by the community. The things that he wanted to do, usually hunting and war, were also the things that his neighbours wanted to do, and if he felt an inclination to become a medicine man he only had to ingratiate himself with some individual already eminent in that profession, and so, in due course, to succeed to his powers of magic. If he was a man of exceptional talent, he might invent some improvement in weapons, or a new skill in hunting. These would not put him into any opposition to the community, but, on the contrary, would be welcomed. The modern man lives a very different life. If he sings in the street he will be thought to be drunk, and if he dances a policeman will reprove him for impeding the traffic. His working day, unless he is exceptionally fortunate, is occupied in a completely monotonous manner in producing something which is valued, not, like the shield of Achilles, as a beautiful piece of work, but mainly for its utility. When his work is over, he cannot, like Milton's Shepherd, 'tell his tale under the hawthorn in the dale,' because there is often no dale anywhere near where he lives, or, if there is, it is full of tins. And always, in our highly regularised way of life, he is obsessed by thoughts of the morrow. Of all the precepts in the Gospels, the one that Christians have most neglected is the commandment to take no thought for the morrow. If he is prudent, thought for the morrow will lead him to save; if he is imprudent, it will make him apprehensive of being unable to pay his debts. In either case the moment loses its savour. Everything is organised, nothing is spontaneous. The Nazis organised 'Strength Through Joy', but joy prescribed by the government is likely to be not very joyful. In those who might otherwise have worthy ambitions, the effect of centralisation is to bring them into competition with too large a number of rivals, and into subjection to an unduly uniform standard of taste. If you wish to be a painter you will not be content to pit yourself against the men with similar desires in your own town; you will go to some school of painting in a metropolis where you will probably conclude that you are mediocre, and having come to this conclusion you may be so discouraged that you are tempted to throw away your paint-brushes and take to money-making or to drink, for a certain degree of self-confidence is essential to achievement. In Renaissance Italy you might have hoped to be the best painter in Siena, and this position would have been quite sufficiently honourable. But you would not now be content to acquire all your training in one small town and pit yourself against your neighbours. We know too much and feel too little. At least we feel too little of those creative emotions from which a good life springs. In regard to what is important we are passive; where we are active it is over trivialities. If life is to be saved from boredom relieved only by disaster, means must be found of restoring individual initiative, not only in things that are trivial, but in the things that really matter. I do not mean that we should destroy those parts of modern organisation upon which the very existence of large populations depends, but I do mean that organisation should be much more flexible, more relieved by local autonomy, and less oppressive to the human spirit through its impersonal vastness, than it has become through its unbearably rapid growth and centralisation, with which our ways of thought and feeling have been able to keep pace.

Lecture 4

THE CONFLICT OF TECHNIQUE AND HUMAN NATURE

Man differs from other animals in many ways. One of these is, that he is willing to engage in activities that are unpleasant in themselves, because they are means to ends that he desires. Animals do things that, from the point of view of the biologist, seem to be labour for a purpose: birds build nests, and beavers build dams. But they do these things from instinct, because they have an impulse to do them, and not because they perceive that they are useful. They do not practise self-control or prudence or foresight or restraint of impulses by the will. Human beings do all these things. When they do more of them than human nature can endure, they suffer a psychological penalty. Part of this penalty is unavoidable in a civilised way of life, but much of it is unnecessary, and could be removed by a different type of social organisation.

Early man had little of this conflict between means and impulses. Hunting, combat, and propagation were necessary for survival and for evolutionary progress, but that was not his reason for engaging in these activities: he engaged in them because they gave him pleasure. Hunting became, in time, an amusement of the idle rich; it had lost its biological usefulness, but remained enjoyable. Combat, of the simple sort directly inspired by impulse, is now only permitted to school-boys, but combativeness remains, and, if denied a better outlet, finds its most important expression in war.

Early man, however, was not wholly without activities that he felt to be useful rather than intrinsically attractive. At a very early stage in human evolution the making of stone implements began, and so inaugurated the long development that led up to our present elaborate economic system. But in the early Stone Age it is possible that the pleasure of artistic creation and of prospective increase of power diffused itself over the laborious stages of the work. When the journey from means to end is not too long, the means themselves are enjoyed if the end is ardently desired. A boy will toil up hill with a toboggan for the sake of the few brief moments of bliss during the descent; no one has to urge him to be industrious, and however he may puff and pant he is still happy. But if instead of the immediate reward you promised him an old-age pension at seventy, his energy would very quickly flag.

Much longer efforts than those of the boy with the toboggan can be inspired by a creative impulse, and still remain spontaneous. A man may spend years of hardship, danger, and poverty in attempts to climb Everest or reach the South Pole or make a scientific discovery, and live all the while as much in harmony with his own impulses as the boy with the toboggan, provided he ardently desires the end and puts his pride into overcoming obstacles. As the Red Indian said, 'there's glory in it'.

The introduction of slavery began the divorce between the purpose of the work and the purposes of the worker. The Pyramids were built for the glory of the Pharaohs; the slaves who did the work had no share in the glory, and worked only from fear of the overseer's lash. Agriculture, when carried on by slaves or serfs, equally brought no direct satisfaction to those who did the work; their satisfaction was only that of being alive and (with luck) free from physical pain.

In modern times before the Industrial Revolution, the diminution of serfdom and the growth of handicrafts increased the number of workers who were their own masters, and who could therefore enjoy some pride in what they produced. It was this state of affairs that gave rise to the type of democracy advocated by Jefferson and the French Revolution, which assumed a vast number of more or less independent producers, as opposed to the huge economic organisations that modern technique has created.

Consider a large factory, say one that makes motor cars. The purpose of the organisation is to make cars, but the purpose of the workers is to earn wages. Subjectively, there is no common purpose. The uniting purpose exists only in owners and managers, and may be completely absent in most of those who do the work. Some may be proud of the excellence of the cars produced, but most, through their unions, are mainly concerned with wages and hours of work.

To a considerable extent, this evil is inseperable from mechanisation combined with large size. Owing to the former, no man makes a large part of a car, but only one small share of some one part; a great deal of work requires little skill, and is completely monotonous. Owing to the latter (the large size of the organisation) the group who collectively make a car have no unity and no sense of solidarity as between management and employees. There is solidarity among the wage-earners, and there may be solidarity in the management. But the solidarity of the wage-earners has no relation to the product; it is concerned to increase wages and diminish hours of work. The management may have a pride in the product, but when an industry is thoroughly commercialised there is a tendency to think only of profit, which may often be secured more easily by advertisement than by improved workmanship.

Two things have led to a diminished pride in workmanship. The earlier was the invention of currency; the later was mass production. Currency led to the valuation of an article by its pride, which is something not intrinsic, but an abstraction shared with other commodities. Things not made to be exchanged may be valued for what they are, not for what they will buy. Cottage gardens in county villages are often lovely, and may have cost much labour, but are not intended to bring any monetary reward. Peasant costumes, which now hardly exist except for the delectation of tourists, were made by their wearers' families, and had no price. The temples of the Acropolis and the medieval cathedrals were not built with any pecuniary motive, and were not capable of being exchanged. Very gradually, a money economy has replaced an economy in which things were produced for the use of the producer, and this change has caused commodities to be viewed as useful rather than delightful.

Mass production has carried this process to new lengths. Suppose you are a manufacturer of buttons: however excellent your buttons may be, you do not want more than a few for your own use. All the rest you wish to exchange for food and shelter, a motor car and your children's education, and so on. These various things share nothing with the buttons except money value. And it is not even the money value of the buttons that is important to you; what is important is profit, i.e. the excess of their selling value above the cost of production, which may be increased by diminishing their intrinsic excellence. Indeed a loss of intrinsic excellence usually results when mass production is substituted for more primitive methods.

There are two consequences of modern organisation, in addition to those already mentioned, that tend to diminish the producer's interest in the product. One is the remoteness of the gain to be expected from the work; the other is the divorce between the management and the worker.

As for the remoteness of the gain: suppose you are engaged at the present time in some subordinate part of the manufacture of some commodity for export – let us say again a motor car. You are told, with much emphasis, that the export drive is necessary in order that we may be able to buy food. The extra food that is bought as a result of your labour does not come to you personally, but is divided among the forty million or so who inhabit Britain. If you are absent from work one day, there is no *visible* harm to the national economy. It is only by an intellectual effort that you can make yourself aware of the harm that you do by not working, and only by a moral effort that you can make yourself do more work than is necessary in order to keep your job. The whole thing is completely different when the need is obvious and pressing, for instance, in a shipwreck. In a shipwreck the crew obey orders without the need of reasoning with themselves, because they have a common purpose which is not remote, and the means to its realisation are not difficult to understand. But if the captain were obliged, like the government, to explain the principles of currency in order to prove his commands wise, the ship would sink before his lecture was finished.

Divorce between the management and the worker has two aspects, one of which is the familiar conflict of capital and labour, while the other is a more general trouble afflicting all large organisations. I do not propose to say anything about the conflict of labour and capital, but the remoteness of government, whether in a political or an economic organisation, whether under capitalism or under socialism, is a somewhat less trite theme, and deserves to be considered.

However society may be organised, there is inevitably a large area of conflict between the general interest and the interest of this or that section. A rise in the price of coal may be advantageous to the coal industry and facilitate an increase in miners' wages, but is disadvantageous to everybody else. When prices and wages are fixed by the government, every decision must disappoint somebody. The considerations which should weigh with the government are so general, and so apparently removed from the everyday life of the workers, that it is very difficult to make them appear cogent. A concentrated advantage is always more readily appreciated than a diffused disadvantage. It is for this sort of reason that governments find it difficult to resist inflation, and that, when they do, they are apt to become unpopular. A government which acts genuinely in the interests of the general public runs a risk of being thought by each section to be perversely ignoring the interests of that section. This is a difficulty which, in a democracy, tends to be increased by every increase in the degree of governmental control.

Moreover, it would be unduly optimistic to expect that governments, even if democratic, will always do what is best in the public interest. I have spoken before of some evils connected with bureaucracy; I wish now to consider those involved in the relation of the official to the public. In a highly organised community those who exercise governmental functions, from Ministers down to the most junior employees in local offices, have their own private interests, which by no means coincide with those of the community. Of these, love of power and dislike of work are the chief. A civil servant who says 'no' to a project satisfies at once his pleasure in exercising authority and his disinclination for effort. And so he comes to seem, and to a certain extent to be, the enemy of those whom he is supposed to serve.

Take, as an illustration, the measures necessary for dealing with a shortage of food. If you possess an allotment, the difficulty of obtaining food may lead you to work hard if you are allowed to use your produce to supplement your rations. But most people must buy all their food unless they are engaged in agriculture. Under *laissez-faire*, prices would soar, and all except the rich would be seriously undernourished. But although this is true, few of us are adequately grateful for the services of the ladies in food offices, and still fewer of them can preserve through fatigue and worry a wholly benevolent attitude to the public. To the public, the ladies appear, however unjustly, as ignorant despots; to the ladies, the public appear as tiresome, fussy, and stupid, perpetually losing things or changing their addresses. It is not easy to see how, out of such a situation, a genuine harmony between government and the governed can be produced.

The ways which have hitherto been discovered of producing a partial harmony between private feelings and public interest have been open to objections of various kinds.

The easiest and most obvious harmoniser is war. In a difficult war, when national self-preservation is in jeopardy, it is easy to induce everybody to work with a will, and if the government is thought competent its orders are readily obeyed. The situation is like that in a shipwreck. But no one would advocate ship-wrecks as means of promoting naval discipline, and we cannot advocate wars on the ground that they cause national unity. No doubt something of the same effect can be produced by the fear of war, but if fear of war is acute for a long enough time it is pretty sure to result in actual war, and while it promotes national unity it also causes both lassitude and hysteria.

Competition, where it exists, is an immensely powerful incentive. It has been generally decried by socialists as one of the evil things in a capitalist society, but the Soviet Government has restored it to a very important place in the organisation of industry. Stakhanovite methods, in which certain workers are rewarded for exceptional proficiency, while others are punished for shortcomings, are a revival of piecework systems against which trade unions have vigorously and successfully campaigned. I have no doubt that these systems have in Russia the merits formerly claimed by capitalists, and the demerits emphasised by trade unions. As a solution of the psychological problem they are certainly inadequate.

But although competition, in many forms, is gravely objectionable, it has, I think, an essential part to play in the promotion of necessary effort, and in some spheres affords a comparatively harmless outlet for the kind of impulses that might otherwise lead to war. No one would advocate the abolition of competition in games. If two hitherto rival football teams, under the influence of brotherly love, decided to cooperate in placing the football first beyond one goal and then beyond the other, no one's happiness would be increased. There is no reason why the zest derived from competition should be confined to athletics. Emulation between teams or localities or organisations can be a useful incentive. But if competition is not to become ruthless and harmful, the penalty for failure must not be disaster, as in war, or starvation, as in unregulated economic competition, but only loss of glory. Football would not be a desirable sport if defeated teams were put to death or left to starve.

In Britain, in recent years, a gallant attempt has been made to appeal to the sense of duty. Austerity is, for the present, unavoidable, and increase of production is the only way out. This is undeniable, and an appeal of this sort is no doubt necessary during a time of crisis. But sense of duty, valuable and indispensable as it may sometimes be, is not a permanent solution, and is not likely to be successful over a long period. It involves a sense of strain, and a constant resistance to natural impulses, which, if continued, must be exhausting and productive of a diminution of natural energy. If it is urged, not on the basis of some simple traditional ethic such as the Ten Commandments, but on complicated economic and political grounds, weariness will lead to scepticism as to the arguments involved, and many people will either become simply indifferent or adopt some probably untrue theory suggesting that there is a short cut to prosperity. Men can be stimulated by hope or driven by fear, but the hope and the fear must be vivid and immediate if they are to be effective without producing weariness.

It is partly for this reason that hysterical propaganda, or at least propaganda intended to cause hysteria, has such widespread influence in the modern world. People are aware, in a general way, that their daily lives are affected by things that happen in distant parts of the world, but they have not the knowledge to understand how this happens, except in the case of a small number of experts. Why is there no rice? Why are bananas so rare? Why have oxen apparently ceased to have tails? If you lay the blame on India, or red tape, or the capitalist system, or the socialist State, you conjure up in people's minds a mythical personified devil whom it is easy to hate. In every misfortune it is a natural impulse to look for an enemy upon whom to lay the blame; savages attribute all illness to hostile magic. Whenever the causes of our troubles are too difficult to be understood, we tend to fall back upon this primitive kind of explanation. A newspaper which offers us a villain to hate is much more appealing than one which goes into all the intricacies of dollar shortages. When the Germans suffered after the first world war, many of them were easily persuaded that the Jews were to blame.

The appeal to hatred of a supposed enemy as the explanation of whatever is painful in our lives is usually destructive and disastrous; it stimulates primitive instinctive energy, but in ways the effects of which are catastrophic. There are various ways of diminishing the potency of appeals to hatred. The best way, obviously, where it is possible, is to cure the evils which cause us to look out for an enemy. Where this cannot be achieved, it may sometimes be possible to disseminate widely a true understanding of the causes that are producing our misfortune. But this is difficult so long as there are powerful forces in politics and in the Press which flourish by the encouragement of hysteria.

I do not think that misfortune, by itself, produces the kind of hysterical hatred that led, for example, to the rise of the Nazis. There has to be a sense of frustration as well as one of misfortune. A Swiss family Robinson, finding plenty to do on their island, will not waste time on hatred. But in a more complex situation the activities that are in fact necessary may be far less capable of making an immediate appeal to individuals. In the present difficult state of British national economy, we know collectively what is needed: increased production, diminished consumption, and stimulation of exports. But these are large general matters, not very visibly related to the welfare of particular men and women. If the activities that are needed on such apparently remote grounds are to be carried out vigorously and cheerfully, ways must be devised of creating some more immediate reason for doing what the national economy requires. This, I think, demands controlled devolution, and opportunities for desirable more or less independent action by individuals or by groups that are not very large.

Democracy, as it exists in large modern States, does not give adequate scope for political initiative except to a tiny minority. We are accustomed to pointing out that what the Greeks called 'democracy' fell short through the exclusion of women and slaves, but we do not always realise that in some important respects it was more democratic than anything that is possible when the governmental area is extensive. Every citizen could vote on every issue; he did not have to delegate his power to a representative. He could elect executive officers, including generals, and could get them condemned if they displeased a majority. The number of citizens was small enough for each man to feel that he counted, and that he could have a significant influence by discussion with his acquaintance. I am not suggesting that this system was good on the whole; it had, in fact, very grave disadvantages. But in the one respect of allowing for individual initiative it was very greatly superior to anything that exists in the modern world.

Consider, for purposes of illustration, the relation of an ordinary taxpayer to an admiral. The taxpayers, collectively, are the admiral's employers. Their agents in Parliament vote his pay, and choose the government which sanctions the authority which appoints the admiral. But if the individual taxpayer were to attempt to assume towards the admiral the attitude of authority which is customary from employer to employee, he would soon be put in his place. The admiral is a great man, accustomed to exercising authority; the ordinary taxpayer is not. In a lesser degree the same sort of thing is true throughout the public services. Even if you only wish to register a letter at a Post Office, the official is in a position of momentary power; he can at least decide when to notice that you desire attention. If you want anything more complicated, he can, if he happens to be in a bad humour, cause you considerable annoyance; he can send you to another man, who may send you back to the first man; and yet both are reckoned 'servants' of the public. The ordinary voter, so far from finding himself the source of all the power of army, navy, police, and civil service, *feels* himself their humble subject, whose duty is, as the Chinese used to say, to 'tremble and obey'. So long as democratic control is remote and rare, while public administration is centralised and authority is delegated from the centre to the circumference, this sense of individual impotence before the powers that be is difficult to avoid. And yet it must be avoided if democracy is to be a reality in feeling and not merely in governmental machinery.

Most of the evils that we have been concerned with in this lecture are no new thing. Ever since the dawn of civilisation most people in civilised communities have led lives full of misery; glory, adventure, initiative were for the privileged few, while for the multitude there was a life of severe toil with occasional harsh cruelty. But the Western nations first, and gradually the whole world, have awakened to a new ideal. We are no longer content that the few should enjoy all the good things while the many are wretched. The evils of early industrialism caused a thrill of horror which they would not have caused in Roman times. Slavery was abolished because it was felt that no human being should be regarded merely as an instrument to the prosperity of another. We no longer attempt, at least in theory, to defend the exploitation of coloured races by white conquerors. Socialism was inspired by the wish to diminish the gap between rich and poor. In all directions, there has been a revolt against injustice and inequality, and an unwillingness to build a brilliant super-structure on a foundation of suffering and degradation.

This new belief is now so generally taken for granted that it is not sufficiently realised how revolutionary it is in the long history of mankind. In this perspective the last hundred and sixty years appear as a continuous revolution inspired by this idea. Like all new beliefs that are influential, it is uncomfortable, and demands difficult adjustments. There is a danger – as there has been with other gospels – lest means should be mistaken for ends, with the result that ends are forgotten. There is a risk that, in the pursuit of equality, good things which there is difficulty in distributing evenly may not be admitted to be good. Some of the unjust societies of the past gave to a minority opportunities which, if we are not careful, the new society that we seek to build may give to no one. When I speak of the evils of the present day, I do so, not to suggest that they are greater than those of the past, but only to make sure that what was good in the past should be carried over into the future, as far as possible unharmed by the transition. But if this is to be achieved, some things must be remembered which are apt to be forgotten in blue-prints of Utopia.

Among the things which are in danger of being unnecessarily sacrificed to democratic equality, perhaps the most important is self-respect. By self-respect I mean the good half of pride – what is called 'proper pride'. The bad half is a sense of superiority. Self-respect will keep a man from being abject when he is in the power of enemies, and will enable him to feel that he may be in the right when the world is against him. If a man has not this quality, he will feel that majority opinion, or governmental opinion, is to be treated as infallible, and such a way of feeling, if it is general, makes both moral and intellectual progress impossible.

Self-respect has been hitherto, of necessity, a virtue of the minority. Wherever there is inequality of power, it is not likely to be found among those who are subject to the rule of others. One of the most revolting features of tyrannies is the way in which they lead the victims of injustice to offer adulation to those who ill-treat them. Roman gladiators saluted the emperors who were about to cause half of them to be slaughtered for amusement. Dostoevski and Bakunin, when in prison, pretended to think well of the Czar Nicholas. Those who are liquidated by the Soviet Government very frequently make an abject confession of sinfulness, while those who escape the purges indulge in nauseous flatteries and not infrequently try to incriminate colleagues. A democratic regime is likely to avoid these grosser forms of self-abasement, and *can* give complete opportunity for the preservation of self-respect. But it *may* do quite the opposite.

Since self-respect has, in the past, been, in the main, confined to the privileged minority, it may easily be undervalued by those who are in opposition to an established oligarchy. And those who believe that the voice of the people is the voice of God may infer that any unusual opinion or peculiar taste is almost a form of impiety, and is to be viewed as a culpable rebellion against the legitimate authority of the herd. This will only be avoided if liberty is as much valued as democracy, and it is realised that a society in which each is the slave of all is only a little better than one in which each is the slave of a despot. There is equality where all are slaves, as well as where all are free. This shows that equality, by itself, is not enough to make a good society.

Perhaps the most important problem in an industrial society, and certainly one of the most difficult, is that of making work interesting, in the sense of being no longer *merely* a means to wages. This is a problem which arises especially in relation to unskilled work. Work that is difficult is likely to be attractive to those who are able to do it. Crossword puzzles and chess are closely analogous to some kinds of skilled work, and yet many people spend much effort on them, merely for pleasure. But with the increase of machinery there is a continual increase in the proportion of wage-earners whose work is completely monotonous and completely easy. Professor Abercrombie, in his *Greater London Plan, 1944*, points out, incidentally and without emphasis, that most modern industries require no specialised aptitudes and therefore need not be sited in districts where traditional skills exist. He says: 'Non-dependence on any one labour pool is further emphasised by the nature of modern work, which demands relatively little skill, but a high degree of steadiness and reliability; these are qualities which can be found almost anywhere among the working class population today.'

'Steadiness and reliability' are certainly very useful qualities, but if they are all that a man's work demands of him, it is not likely that he will find his work interesting, and it is pretty certain that such satisfaction as his life may offer him will have to be found outside working hours. I do not believe that this is wholly unavoidable, even when the work is in itself monotonous and uninteresting.

The first requisite is to restore to the worker some of the feelings connected in the past with ownership. Actual ownership by an individual worker is not possible when machinery is involved, but there can be ways of securing the kind of pride associated with the feeling that this is 'my' work, or at any rate 'our' work, where 'our' refers to a group small enough to know each other and have an active sense of solidarity. This is not secured by nationalisation, which leaves managers and officials almost as remote from the workers as they are under a capitalist regime. What is needed is local small-scale democracy in all internal affairs; foremen and managers should be elected by those over whom they are to have authority.

The impersonal and remote character of those in authority over an industrial undertaking is fatal to any proprietorial interest on the part of the ordinary employee. Mr Burnham's 'Managerial Revolution' presents a far from cheerful picture of the possibilities in the near future. If we wish to avoid the drab world that he prophesies, the thing of first importance is to democratise management. This subject is dealt with admirably in Mr James Gillespie's *Free Expression in Industry*, and I cannot do better than quote from him. He says:

> There is a sense of frustration when an individual or a group has a serious problem and cannot get to the top with it. As in civil bureaucracy, so it is in industrial bureaucracy – there are the same delays, the reference to X or Y, the statement of the rules and the same feeling of helplessness and frustration. 'If I could only get to the chief, he would know, he would see . . .' This desire to get to the top is very real and very important. The monthly meeting of representatives of employee groups is not without value, but it is not an effective substitute for a face-to-face relationship between owner and employee. It does not help this situation when a shop steward, or an operator, goes to the foreman with a problem and the foreman, shorn of authority, through transfer of controls, can do nothing but pass it on to the superintendent. He, in turn, passes it to the works manager who puts it on the agenda for the next meeting. Or the matter may be referred to the welfare department, a big department in a big company, and a substitute for the welfare or personnel manager, himself a substitute for one role of managing director or owner, deals with it or passes it on.
>
> In the large company there is more than a sense of frustration; there is a peculiar meaninglessness about its operations to the member of the rank and file. He knows little of the significance of his job in the company as a whole. He does not know who is the real boss; he frequently does not know who is

the General Manager, and, often enough, he has never been spoken to by the head Works Manager. The Sales Manager, the Cost Manager, the Planning Manager, the Chief Welfare Manager and many others, are just people with good jobs and short hours. He has no part with them, they do not belong to his group.

Democracy, whether in politics or in industry, is not a psychological reality so long as the government or the management is regarded as 'they', a remote body which goes its lordly way and which it is natural to regard with hostility – a hostility that is impotent unless it takes the form of rebellion. In industry, as Mr Gillespie points out, very little has been done in this direction, and management is, with rare exceptions, frankly monarchical or oligarchic. This is an evil which, if left unchecked, tends to increase with every increase in the size of organisations.

Ever since history began, the majority of mankind have lived under a load of poverty and suffering and cruelty, and have felt themselves impotent under the sway of hostile or coldly impersonal powers. These evils are no longer necessary to the existence of civilisation; they can be removed by the help of modern science and modern technique, provided these are used in a humane spirit and with an understanding of the springs of life and happiness. Without such understanding, we may inadvertently create a new prison, just, perhaps, since none will be outside it, but dreary and joyless and spiritually dead. How such a disaster is to be averted, I shall consider in my last two lectures.

POSTSCRIPT

An interesting and painful example of the decay of quality through modern machine methods is afforded by the Scottish tweed industry. Hand-woven tweeds, universally acknowledged to be of superlative excellence, have long been produced in the Highlands, the Hebrides and the Orkney and Shetland Islands, but the competition of machine-woven tweeds has hit the hand-weavers very hard, and the purchase tax, according to debates in both Houses of Parliament, is giving them their *coup de grâce*. The result is that those who can no longer make a living by exercising their craft are compelled to leave the islands and Highlands to live in cities or even to emigrate.

Against the short-term economic gain of a purchase tax which brings in from £1,000,000 to £1,500,000 a year must be placed long-term losses which are hardly calculable.

First, there is the loss, added to those we have already suffered in the blind and greedy heyday of the Industrial Revolution, of one more local and traditional skill, which has brought to those who exercised it the joy of craftsmanship and a way of life which, though hard, gave pride and self-respect and the joy of achievement, through ingenuity and effort, in circumstances of difficulty and risk.

Secondly, there is the diminution in the intrinsic excellence of the product, both aesthetic and utilitarian.

Thirdly, this murder of a local industry aggravates the tendency to uncontrollable growth of cities, which we are attempting in our national town planning to avoid. The independent weavers become units in a vast, hideous and unhealthy human ant-hill. Their economic security is no longer dependent on their own skill and upon the forces of nature. It is lost in a few large organisations, in which if one fails all fail, and the causes of failure cannot be understood.

Two factors make this process – a microcosm of the Industrial Revolution – inexcusable at this date. On the one hand, unlike the early industrialists, who could not see the consequences of their own acts, we know the resultant evils all too well. On the other hand, these evils are no longer necessary for the increase of production, or for the raising of the material standards of living of the worker. Electricity and motor-transport have made small units of industry not only economically permissible but even desirable, for they obviate immense expenditure on transportation and organisation. Where a rural industry still flourishes, it should be gradually mechanised, but be left in situ and in small units.

In those parts of the world in which industrialism is still young, the possibility of avoiding the horrors we have experienced still exists. India, for example, is traditionally a land of village communities. It would be a tragedy if this traditional way of life with all its evils were to be suddenly and violently exchanged for the greater evils of urban industrialism, as they would apply to people whose standard of living is already pitifully low. Gandhi, realising these dangers, attempted to put the clock back by reviving hand-loom weaving throughout the continent. He was half right, but it is folly to reject the advantages that science gives us; instead they should be seized with eagerness and applied to increase the material wealth and, at the same time, to preserve these simple privileges of pure air, of status in a small community, of pride in responsibility and work well done, which are rarely possible for the worker in a large industrial town. The rivers of the Himalayas should provide all the hydro-electric power that is needed for the gradual mechanisation of the village industries of India and for immeasurable improvement of physical well-being, without either the obvious disaster of industrial slump or the more subtle loss and degradation which results when age-old traditions are too rudely broken.

Lecture 5

CONTROL AND INITIATIVE: THEIR RESPECTIVE SPHERES

A healthy and progressive society requires both central control and individual and group initiative: without control there is anarchy, and without initiative there is stagnation. I want in this lecture to arrive at some general principles as to what matters should be controlled and what should be left to private or semi-private initiative. Some of the qualities that we should wish to find in a community are in their essence static, while others are by their very nature dynamic. Speaking very roughly, we may expect the static qualities to be suitable for governmental control, while the dynamic qualities should be promoted by the initiative of individuals or groups. But if such initiative is to be possible, and if it is to be fruitful rather than destructive, it will need to be fostered by appropriate institutions, and the safeguarding of such institutions will have to be one of the functions of government. It is obvious that in a state of anarchy there could not be universities or scientific research or publication of books, or even such simple things as seaside holidays. In our complex world, there cannot be fruitful initiative without government, but unfortunately there can be government without initiative.

The *primary* aims of government, I suggest, should be three: security, justice, and conservation. These are things of the utmost importance to human happiness, and they are things which only government can bring about. At the same time, no one of them is absolute; each may, in some circumstances, have to be sacrificed in some degree for the sake of a greater degree of some other good. I shall say something about each in turn.

Security, in the sense of protection of life and property, has always been recognised as one of the primary purposes of the State. Many States, however, while safeguarding law-abiding citizens against other citizens, have not thought it necessary to protect them against the State. Wherever there is arrest by administrative order, and punishment without due process of law, private people have no security, however firmly the State may be established. And even insistence on due process of law is insufficient, unless the judges are independent of the executive. This order of ideas was to the fore in the seventeenth and eighteenth centuries, under the slogan 'liberty of the subject' or 'rights of man'. But the 'liberty' and the 'rights' that were sought could only be secured by the State, and then only if the State was of the kind that is called 'Liberal'. It is only in the West that this liberty and these rights have been secured.

To inhabitants of Western countries in the present day, a more interesting kind of security is security against attacks by hostile States. This is more interesting because it has not been secured, and because it becomes more important year by year as methods of warfare develop. This kind of security will only become possible when there is a single world government with a monopoly of all the major weapons of war. I shall not enlarge upon this subject, since it is somewhat remote from my theme. I will only say, with all possible emphasis, that unless and until mankind have achieved the security of a single government for the world, everything else of value, of no matter what kind, is precarious, and may at any moment be destroyed by war.

Economic security has been one of the most important aims of modern British legislation. Insurance against unemployment, sickness, and destitution in old age, has removed from the lives of wage-earners a great deal of painful uncertainty as to their future. Medical security has been promoted by measures which have greatly increased the average length of life and diminished the amount of illness. Altogether, life in Western countries, apart from war, is very much less dangerous than it was in the eighteenth century, and this change is mainly due to various kinds of governmental control.

Security, though undoubtedly a good thing, may be sought excessively and become a fetish. A secure life is not necessarily a happy life; it may be rendered dismal by boredom and monotony. Many people, especially while they are young, welcome a spice of dangerous adventure, and may even find relief in war as an escape from humdrum safety. Security by itself is a negative aim inspired by fear; a satisfactory life must have a positive aim inspired by hope. This sort of adventurous hope involves risk and therefore fear. But fear deliberately chosen is not such an evil thing as fear forced upon a man by outward circumstances. We cannot therefore be content with security alone, or imagine that it can bring the millennium.

And now as to justice:

Justice, especially economic justice, has become, in quite recent times, a governmental purpose. Justice has come to be interpreted as equality, except where exceptional merit is thought to deserve an exceptional but still moderate reward. Political justice, i.e. democracy, has been aimed at since the American and French Revolutions, but economic justice is a newer aim, and requires a much greater amount of governmental control. It is held by Socialists, rightly, in my opinion, to involve State ownership of key industries and considerable regulation of foreign trade. Opponents of Socialism may argue that economic justice can be too dearly bought, but no one can deny that, if it is to be achieved, a very large amount of State control over industry and finance is essential.

There are, however, limits to economic justice which are, at least tacitly, acknowledged by even the most ardent of its Western advocates. For example, it is of the utmost importance to seek out ways of approaching economic equality by improving the position of the less fortunate parts of the world, not only because there is an immense sum of unhappiness to be relieved, but also because the world cannot be stable or secure against great wars while glaring inequalities persist. But an attempt to bring about economic equality between Western nations and South-east Asia, by any but gradual methods, would drag the more prosperous nations down to the level of the less prosperous, without any appreciable advantage to the latter.

Justice, like security, but to an even greater degree, is a principle which is subject to limitations. There is justice where all are equally poor as well as where all are equally rich, but it would seem fruitless to make the rich poorer if this was not going to make the poor richer. The case against justice is even stronger if, in the pursuit of equality, it is going to make even the poor poorer than before. And this might well happen if a general lowering of education and a diminution of fruitful research were involved. If there had not been economic injustice in Egypt and Babylon, the art of writing would never have been invented. There is, however, no *necessity*, with modern methods of production, to perpetuate economic injustice in industrially developed nations in order to promote progress in the arts of civilisation. There is only a danger to be born in mind, not, as in the past, a technical impossibility.

I come now to my third head, conservation.

Conservation, like security and justice, demands action by the State. I mean by 'conservation' not only the preservation of ancient monuments and beauty-spots, the upkeep of roads and public utilities, and so on. These things are done at present, except in time of war. What I have chiefly in mind is the preservation of the world's natural resources. This is a matter of enormous importance, to which very little attention has been paid. During the past hundred and fifty years mankind has used up the raw materials of industry and the soil upon which agriculture depends, and this wasteful expenditure of natural capital has proceeded with ever-increasing velocity. In relation to industry, the most striking example is oil. The amount of accessible oil in the world is unknown, but is certainly not unlimited; already the need for it has reached the point at which there is a risk of its contributing to bringing about a third world war. When oil is no longer available in large quantities, a great deal will have to be changed in our way of life. If we try to substitute atomic energy, that will only result in exhaustion of the available supplies of uranium and thorium. Industry as it exists at present depends essentially upon the expenditure of natural capital, and cannot long continue in its present prodigal fashion.

Even more serious, according to some authorities, is the situation in regard to agriculture, as set forth with great vividness in Mr Vogt's *Road to Survival*. Except in a few favoured areas (of which Western Europe is one), the prevailing methods of cultivating the soil rapidly exhaust its fertility. The growth of the Dust Bowl in America is the best known example of a destructive process which is going on in most parts of the world. As, meantime, the population increases, a disastrous food shortage is inevitable within the next fifty years unless drastic steps are taken. The necessary measures are known to students of agriculture, but only governments can take them, and then only if they are willing and able to face unpopularity. This is a problem which has received far too little attention. It must be faced by anyone who hopes for a stable world without internecine wars – wars which, if they are to ease the food shortage, must be far more destructive than those we have already endured, for during both the world wars the population of the world increased. This question of a reform in agriculture is perhaps the most important that the governments of the near future will have to face, except the prevention of war.

I have spoken of security, justice, and conservation as the most essential of governmental functions, because these are things that only governments can bring about. I have not meant to suggest that governments should have no other functions. But in the main their functions in other spheres should be to encourage non-governmental initiative, and to create opportunities for its exercise in beneficent ways. There are anarchic and criminal forms of initiative which cannot be tolerated in a civilised society. There are other forms of initiative, such as that of the well-established inventor, which everybody recognises to be useful. But there is a larger intermediate class of innovators of whose activities it cannot be known in advance whether the effects will be good or bad. It is particularly in relation to this uncertain class that it is necessary to urge the desirability of freedom to experiment, for this class includes all that has been best in the history of human achievement.

Uniformity, which is a natural result of State control, is desirable in some things and undesirable in others. In Florence, in the days before Mussolini, there was one rule of the roads in the town and the opposite rule in the surrounding country. This kind of diversity was inconvenient, but there were many matters in which Fascism suppressed a *desirable* kind of diversity. In matters of opinion it is a good thing if there is vigorous discussion between different schools of thought. In the mental world there is everything to be said in favour of a struggle for existence, leading, with luck, to a survival of the fittest. But if there is to be mental competition, there must be ways of limiting the means to be employed. The decision should not be by war, or by assassination, or by imprisonment of those holding certain opinions, or by preventing those holding unpopular views from earning a living. Where private enterprise prevails, or where there are many small States, as in Renaissance Italy and eighteenth-century Germany, these conditions are to some extent fulfilled by rivalry between different possible patrons. But when, as has tended to happen throughout Europe, States become large and private fortunes small, traditional methods of securing intellectual diversity fail. The only method that remains available is for the State to hold the ring and establish some sort of Queensbury rules by which the contest is to be conducted.

Artists and writers are nowadays almost the only people who may with luck exercise a powerful and important initiative as individuals, and not in connection with some group. While I lived in California, there were two men who set to work to inform the world as to the condition of migrant labour in that State. One, who was a novelist, dealt with the theme in a novel; the other, who was a teacher in a State university, dealt with it in a careful piece of academic research. The novelist made a fortune; the teacher was dismissed from his post, and suffered an imminent risk of destitution.

But the initiative of the writer, though as yet it survives, is threatened in various ways. If book-production is in the hands of the State, as it is in Russia, the State can decide what shall be published, and, unless it delegates its power to some completely non-partisan authority, there is a likelihood that no books will appear except such as are pleasing to leading politicians. The same thing applies, of course, to newspapers. In this sphere, uniformity would be a disaster, but would be a very probable result of unrestricted State socialism.

Men of science, as I pointed out in my third lecture, could formerly work in isolation, as writers still can; Cavendish and Faraday and Mendel depended hardly at all upon institutions, and Darwin only in so far as the government enabled him to share the voyage of the *Beagle*. But this isolation is a thing of the past. Most research requires expensive apparatus; some kinds require the financing of expeditions to difficult regions. Without facilities provided by a government or a university, few men can achieve much in modern science. The conditions which determine who is to have access to such facilities are therefore of great importance. If only those are eligible who are considered orthodox in current controversies, scientific progress will soon cease, and will give way to a scholastic reign of authority such as stifled science throughout the Middle Ages.

In politics, the association of personal initiative with a group is obvious and essential. Usually two groups are involved: the party and the electorate. If you wish to carry some reform, you must first persuade your party to adopt the reform, and then persuade the electorate to adopt your party. You may, of course, be able to operate directly upon the Government, but this is seldom possible in a matter that rouses much public interest. When it is not possible, the initiative required involves so much energy and time, and is so likely to end in failure, that most people prefer to acquiesce in the *status quo*, except to the extent of voting, once in five years, for some candidate who promises reform.

In a highly organised world, personal initiative connected with a group must be confined to a few unless the group is small. If you are a member of a small committee you may reasonably hope to influence its decisions. In national politics, where you are one of some twenty million voters, your influence is infinitesimal unless you are exceptional or occupy an exceptional position. You have, it is true, a twenty-millionth share in the government of others, but only a twenty-millionth share in the government of yourself. You are therefore much more conscious of being governed than of governing. The government becomes in your thoughts a remote and largely malevolent 'they', not a set of men whom you, in concert with others, who share your opinions, have chosen to carry out your wishes. Your individual feeling about politics, in these circumstances, is not that intended to be brought about by democracy, but much more nearly what it would be under a dictatorship.

The sense of bold adventure, and of capacity to bring about results that are felt to be important, can only be restored if power can be delegated to small groups in which the individual is not overwhelmed by mere numbers. A considerable degree of central control is indispensable, if only for the reasons that we considered at the beginning of this lecture. But to the utmost extent compatible with this requisite, there should be devolution of the powers of the State to various kinds of bodies – geographical, industrial, cultural, according to their functions. The powers of these bodies should be sufficient to make them interesting, and to cause energetic men to find satisfaction in influencing them. They would need, if they were to fulfil their purpose, a considerable measure of financial autonomy. Nothing is so damping and deadening to initiative as to have a carefully thought out scheme vetoed by a central authority which knows almost nothing about it and has no sympathy with its objects. Yet this is what constantly happens in Britain under our system of centralised control. Something more elastic and less rigid is needed if the best brains are not to be paralysed. And it must be an essential feature of any wholesome system that as much as possible of the power should be in the hands of men who are interested in the work that is to be done.

The problem of delimiting the powers of various bodies will, of course, be one presenting many difficulties. The general principle should be to leave to smaller bodies all functions which do not prevent the larger bodies from fulfilling their purpose. Confining ourselves, for the moment, to geographical bodies, there should be a hierarchy from the world government to parish councils. The function of the world government is to prevent war, and it should have only such powers as are necessary to this end. This involves a monopoly of armed force, a power to sanction and revise treaties, and the right to give decisions in disputes between States. But the world government should not interfere with the internal affairs of member States, except in so far as is necessary to secure the observance of treaties. In like manner the national government should leave as much as possible to County Councils, and they in turn to Borough and Parish Councils. A short-run loss of efficiency may be expected in some respects, but if the functions of subordinate bodies are made sufficiently important able men will find satisfaction in belonging to them, and the temporary loss of efficiency will soon be more than made good.

At present local government is too generally regarded as the hobby of the well-to-do and the retired, since as a rule only they have leisure to devote to it. Because they are unable to participate, few young and able men and women take much interest in the affairs of their local community. If this is to be remedied, local government must become a paid career, for the same reasons as have led to the payment of Members of Parliament.

Whether an organisation is geographical or cultural or ideological, it will always have two sorts of relations, those to its own members, and those to the outside world. The relations of a body to its own members should, as a rule, be left to the free decision of the members, so long as there is no infringement of the law. Although the relations of a body to its members should be decided by the members, there are some principles which, if democracy is to have any reality, it is to be hoped that the members will bear in mind. Take, for example, a large business. The attack upon capitalism by Socialists has been concerned, perhaps too exclusively, with questions of income rather than with questions of power. When an industry is transferred to the State by nationalisation it may happen that there is still just as much inequality of power as there was in the days of private capitalism, the only change being that the holders of power are now officials, not owners. It is, of course, unavoidable that in any large organisation there should be executive officers who have more power than the rank and file, but it is very desirable that such inequality of power should be no greater than is absolutely necessary, and that as much initiative as possible should be distributed to all members of the organisation. In this connection a very interesting book is Mr John Spedan Lewis's *Partnership For All − A 34-year Old Experiment in Industrial Democracy*. What makes the book interesting is that it is based upon a long and extensive practical experience by a man who combines public spirit with experimental boldness. On the financial side he has made all the workers in his enterprises partners who share in the profit, but, in addition to this financial innovation, he has taken pains to give to each employee a feeling that he shares actively in the government of the whole enterprise, though I doubt whether, by his methods, it is possible to go as far as we ought to go towards democracy in industry. He has also developed a technique for giving important posts to the men most capable of carrying on the work involved. It is interesting to observe that he has arguments against equality of remuneration, not only on the ground that those who do difficult work deserve better pay, but, on the converse ground, that better pay is a cause of better work. He says: 'It is quite false to imagine that ability and the will to use it are both of them what mathematicians call, I believe, "constants" and that all that varies is the income that the worker happens to get in return. Not only your will to do your best but your actual ability depends very largely upon what you are paid. Not only are people highly paid because they are able; they are also able because they are highly paid.'

This principle has a wider application than Mr Lewis gives it, and it applies not only to pay but also to honour and status. I think, in fact, that the chief value of an increase of salary lies in increase of status. A scientific worker whose work is generally acclaimed as important will get the same stimulus from recognition as a man in another field might get from an increase of income. The important thing, in fact, is hopefulness and a certain kind of buoyancy, a thing in which Europe has become very deficient as a result of the two World Wars. Freedom of enterprise, in the old *laissez-faire* sense, is no longer to be advocated, but it is of the utmost importance that there should still be freedom of initiative, and that able men should find scope for their ability.

This, however, is only one side of what is desirable in a large organisation. The other thing that is important is that those in control should not be possessed of too absolute a power over the others. For centuries reformers fought against the power of kings, and then they set to work to fight against the power of capitalists. Their victory in this second contest will be fruitless if it merely results in replacing the power of the capitalists by the power of the officials. Of course there are practical difficulties, because officials must often take decisions without waiting for the slow results of a democratic process, but there should always be possibilities, on the one hand, of deciding general lines of policy democratically, and, on the other hand, of criticising the actions of officials without fear of being penalised for so doing. Since it is natural to energetic men to love power, it may be assumed that officials in the great majority of cases will wish to have more power than they ought to have. There is, therefore, in every large organisation the same need of democratic watchfulness as there is in the political sphere.

The relations of an organisation to the outside world are a different matter. They ought not to be decided merely on grounds of power, that is to say, on the bargaining strength of the organisation in question, but should be referred to a neutral authority whenever they cannot be settled by friendly negotiation. To this principle there should be no exception until we come to the world as a whole, which, so far, has no external political relations. If a Wellsian War of the Worlds were possible, we should need an Inter-Planetary Authority.

Differences between nations, so long as they do not lead to

hostility, are by no means to be deplored. Living for a time in a foreign country makes us aware of merits in which our own country is deficient, and this is true whichever country our own may be. The same thing holds of differences between different regions within one country, and of the differing types produced by different professions. Uniformity of character and uniformity of culture are to be regretted. Biological evolution has depended upon inborn differences between individuals or tribes, and cultural evolution depends upon acquired differences. When these disappear, there is no longer any material for selection. In the modern world, there is a real danger of too great similarity between one region and another in cultural respects. One of the best ways of minimising this evil is an increase in the autonomy of different groups.

The general principle which, if I am right, should govern the respective spheres of authority and initiative, may be stated broadly in terms of the different kinds of impulses that make up human nature. On the one hand, we have impulses to hold what we possess, and (too often) to acquire what others possess. On the other hand, we have creative impulses, impulses to put something into the world which is not taken away from anybody else. These may take humble forms, such as cottage gardens, or may represent the summit of human achievement, as in Shakespeare and Newton. Broadly speaking, the regularising of possessive impulses and their control by the law belong to the *essential* functions of government, while the creative impulses, though governments may encourage them, should derive their main influence from individual or group autonomy.

Material goods are more a matter of possession than goods that are mental. A man who eats a piece of food prevents everyone else from eating it, but a man who writes or enjoys a poem does not prevent another man from writing or enjoying one just as good or better. That is why, in regard to material goods, justice is important, but in regard to mental goods the thing that is needed is opportunity and an environment that makes hope of achievement seem rational. It is not great material rewards that stimulate men capable of creative work; few poets or men of science have made fortunes or wished to do so. Socrates was put to death by Authority, but he remained completely placid in his last moments because he had done his work. If he had been loaded with honours but prevented from doing his work, he would have felt that he had suffered a far severer penalty. In a monolithic State, where Authority controls all the means of publicity, a man of marked originality is likely to suffer this worse fate: whether or not he is subjected to legal penalties, he is unable to make his ideas known. When this happens in a community, it cannot any longer contribute anything of value to the collective life of mankind.

The control of greedy or predatory impulses is imperatively necessary, and therefore States, and even a World State, are needed for survival. But we cannot be content merely to be alive rather than dead; we wish to live happily, vigorously, creatively. For this the State can provide a part of the necessary conditions, but only if it does not, in the pursuit of security, stifle the largely unregulated impulses which give life its savour and its value. The individual life still has its due place, and must not be subjected too completely to the control of vast organisations. To guard against this danger is very necessary in the world that modern technique has created.

Lecture 6

INDIVIDUAL AND SOCIAL ETHICS

In this last lecture I wish to do two things. First, to repeat briefly the conclusions reached in earlier lectures; second, to relate social and political doctrines to the individual ethics by which a man should guide his personal life, and after the evils we have recognised and the dangers that we have acknowledged, to hold out nevertheless, as resulting from our survey, certain high hopes for the not too distant future of mankind, which I, for my part, believe to be justified on a sober estimate of possibilities.

To begin with recapitulation. Broadly speaking, we have distinguished two main purposes of social activities: on the one hand, security and justice require centralized governmental control, which must extend to the creation of a world government if it is to be effective. Progress, on the contrary, requires the utmost scope for personal initiative that is compatible with social order.

The method of securing as much as possible of both these aims is *devolution*. The world government must leave national governments free in everything not involved in the prevention of war; national governments, in their turn, must leave as much scope as possible to local authorities. In industry, it must not be thought that all problems are solved when there is nationalisation. A large industry – e.g. railways – should have a large measure of self-government; the relation of employees to the State in a nationalised industry should not be a mere reproduction of their former relation to private employers. Everything concerned with opinion, such as newspapers, books, and political propaganda, must be left to genuine competition, and carefully safeguarded from governmental control, as well as from every other form of monopoly. But the competition must be cultural and intellectual, not economic, and still less military or by means of the criminal law.

In cultural matters, diversity is a condition of progress. Bodies that have a certain independence of the State, such as universities and learned societies, have great value in this respect. It is deplorable to see, as in present-day Russia, men of science compelled to subscribe to obscurantist nonsense at the behest of scientifically ignorant politicians who are able and willing to enforce their ridiculous decisions by the use of economic and police power. Such pitiful spectacles can only be prevented by limiting the activities of politicians to the sphere in which they may be supposed competent. They should not presume to decide what is good music, or good biology, or good philosophy. I should not wish such matters to be decided in this country by the personal taste of any Prime Minister, past, present, or future, even if, by good luck, his taste were impeccable.

I come now to the question of personal ethics, as opposed to the question of social and political institutions. No man is wholly free, and no man is wholly a slave. To the extent to which a man has freedom, he needs a personal morality to guide his conduct. There are some who would say that a man need only obey the accepted moral code of his community. But I do not think any student of anthropology could be content with this answer. Such practices as cannibalism, human sacrifice, and head hunting have died out as a result of moral protests against conventional moral opinion. If a man seriously desires to live the best life that is open to him, he must learn to be critical of the tribal customs and tribal beliefs that are generally accepted among his neighbours.

But in regard to departures, on conscientious grounds, from what is thought right by the society to which a man belongs, we must distinguish between the authority of custom and the authority of law. Very much stronger grounds are needed to justify an action which is illegal than to justify one which only contravenes conventional morality. The reason is that respect for law is an indispensable condition for the existence of any tolerable social order. When a man considers a certain law to be bad, he has a right, and may have a duty, to try to get it changed, but it is only in rare cases that he does right to break it. I do not deny that there are situations in which law-breaking becomes a duty: it is a duty when a man profoundly believes that it would be a sin to obey. This covers the case of the conscientious objector. Even if you are quite convinced that he is mistaken, you cannot say that he ought not to act as his conscience dictates. When legislators are wise, they avoid, as far as possible, framing laws in such a way as to compel conscientious men to choose between sin and what is legally a crime.

I think it must also be admitted that there are cases in which revolution is justifiable. There are cases where the legal government is so bad that it is worth while to overthrow it by force in spite of the risk of anarchy that is involved. This risk is very real. It is noteworthy that the most successful revolutions – that of England in 1688 and that of America in 1776 – were carried out by men who were deeply imbued with a respect for law. Where this is absent, revolution is apt to lead to either anarchy or dictatorship. Obedience to the law, therefore, though not an *absolute* principle, is one to which great weight must be attached, and to which exceptions should only be admitted in rare cases after mature consideration.

We are led by such problems to a deep duality in ethics, which, however perplexing, demands recognition.

Throughout recorded history, ethical beliefs have had two very different sources, one political, the other concerned with personal religious and moral convictions. In the Old Testament the two appear quite separately, one as the Law, the other as the Prophets. In the Middle Ages there was the same kind of distinction between the official morality inculcated by the hierarchy and the personal holiness that was taught and practised by the great mystics. This duality of personal and civic morality, which still persists, is one of which any adequate ethical theory must take account. Without civic morality communities perish; without personal morality their survival has no value. Therefore civic and personal morality are equally necessary to a good world.

Ethics is not concerned *solely* with duty to my neighbour, however rightly such duty may be conceived. The performance of public duty is not the whole of what makes a good life; there is also the pursuit of private excellence. For man, though partly social, is not wholly so. He has thoughts and feelings and impulses which may be wise or foolish, noble or base, filled with love or inspired by hate. And for the better among these thoughts and feelings and impulses, if his life is to be tolerable, there must be scope. For although few men can be happy in solitude, still fewer can be happy in a community which allows no freedom of individual action.

Individual excellence, although a great part of it consists in right behaviour towards other people, has also another aspect. If you neglect your duties for the sake of trivial amusement, you will have pangs of conscience; but if you are tempted away for a time by great music or a fine sunset, you will return with no sense of shame and no feeling that you have been wasting your

time. It is dangerous to allow politics and social duty to dominate too completely our conception of what constitutes individual
excellence. What I am trying to convey, although it is not
dependent upon any theological belief, is in close harmony with
Christian ethics. Socrates and the Apostles laid it down that we
ought to obey God rather than man, and the Gospels enjoin love
of God as emphatically as love of our neighbours. All great
religious leaders, and also all great artists and intellectual
discoverers, have shown a sense of moral compulsion to fulfil
their creative impulses, and a sense of moral exaltation when
they have done so. This emotion is the basis of what the Gospels
call duty to God, and is (I repeat) separable from theological
belief. Duty to my neighbour, at any rate as my neighbour
conceives it, may not be the whole of my duty. If I have a
profound conscientious conviction that I ought to act in a way
that is condemned by governmental authority, I ought to follow
my conviction. And conversely, society ought to allow me
freedom to follow my convictions except when there are very
powerful reasons for restraining me.

But it is not only acts inspired by a sense of duty that should
be free from excessive social pressure. An artist or a scientific
discoverer may be doing what is of most social utility, but he
cannot do his proper work from a sense of duty alone. He must
have a spontaneous impulse to paint or to discover, for, if not, his
painting will be worthless and his discoveries unimportant.

The sphere of individual action is not to be regarded as ethic-
ally inferior to that of social duty. On the contrary, some of the
best of human activities are, at least in feeling, rather personal
than social. As I said in Lecture III, prophets, mystics, poets,
scientific discoverers, are men whose lives are dominated by a
vision; they are essentially solitary men. When their dominant
impulse is strong, they feel that they cannot obey authority if it
runs counter to what they profoundly believe to be good.
Although, on this account, they are often persecuted in their

own day, they are apt to be, of all men, those to whom posterity pays the highest honour. It is such men who put into the world the things that we most value, not only in religion, in art, and in science, but also in our way of feeling towards our neighbour, for improvements in the sense of social obligation, as in everything else, have been largely due to solitary men whose thoughts and emotions were not subject to the dominion of the herd.

If human life is not to become dusty and uninteresting it is important to realise that there are things that have a value which is quite independent of utility. What is useful because it is a means of something else, and the something else, if it is not in turn merely a means, must be valued for its own sake, for otherwise the usefulness is illusory.

To strike the right balance between ends and means is both difficult and important. If you are concerned to emphasise means, you may point out that the difference between a civilised man and a savage, between an adult and a child, between a man and an animal, consists largely in a difference as to the weight attached to ends and means in conduct. A civilised man insures his life, a savage does not; an adult brushes his teeth to prevent decay, a child does not except under compulsion; men labour in the fields to provide food for the winter, animals do not. Forethought, which involves doing unpleasant things now for the sake of pleasant things in the future, is one of the most essential marks of mental development. Since forethought is difficult and requires control of impulse, moralists stress its necessity, and lay more stress on the virtue of present sacrifice than on the pleasantness of the subsequent reward. You must do right because it is right, and not because it is the way to get to heaven. You must save because all sensible people do, and not because you may ultimately secure an income that will enable you to enjoy life. And so on.

But the man who wishes to emphasise ends rather than means may advance contrary arguments with equal truth. It is pathetic to see an elderly rich business man, who from work and worry in youth has become dyspeptic, so that he can eat only dry toast and drink only water while his careless guests feast; the joys of wealth, which he had anticipated throughout long laborious years, elude him, and his only pleasure is the use of financial power to compel his sons to submit in their turn to a similar futile drudgery. Misers, whose absorption in means is pathological, are generally recognised to be unwise, but minor forms of the same malady are apt to receive undue commendation. Without some consciousness of ends, life becomes dismal and colourless; ultimately the need for excitement too often finds a worse outlet than it would otherwise have done, in war or cruelty or intrigue or some other destructive activity.

Men who boast of being what is called 'practical' are for the most part exclusively preoccupied with means. But theirs is only one-half of wisdom. When we take account of the other half, which is concerned with ends, the economic process and the whole of human life take on an entirely new aspect. We ask no longer: what have the producers produced, and what has consumption enabled the consumers in their turn to produce? We ask instead: what has there been in the lives of consumers and producers to make them glad to be alive? What have they felt or known or done that could justify their creation? Have they experienced the glory of new knowledge? Have they known love and friendship? Have they rejoiced in sunshine and the spring and the smell of flowers? Have they felt the joy of life that simple communities express in dance and song? Once in Los Angeles I was taken to see the Mexican colony – idle vagabonds, I was told, but to me they seemed to be enjoying more of what makes life a boon and not a curse than fell to the lot of my anxious hard-working hosts. When I tried to explain this feeling, however, I was met with a blank and total lack of comprehension.

People do not always remember that politics, economics, and social organisation generally, belong in the realm of means, not ends. Our political and social thinking is prone to what may be called the 'administrator's fallacy', by which I mean the habit of looking upon a society as a systematic whole, of a sort that is thought good if it is pleasant to contemplate as a model of order, a planned organism with parts neatly dove-tailed into each other. But a society does not, or at least should not, exist to satisfy an external survey, but to bring a good life to the individuals who compose it. It is in the individuals, not in the whole, that ultimate value is to be sought. A good society is a means to a good life for those who compose it, not something having a separate kind of excellence on its own account.

When it is said that a nation is an organism, an analogy is being used which may be dangerous if its limitations are not recognised. Men and the higher animals are organisms in a strict sense: whatever good or evil befalls a man befalls him as a single person, not this or that part of him. If I have toothache, or a pain in my toe, it is I that have the pain, and it would not exist if no nerves connected the part concerned with my brain. But when a farmer in Herefordshire is caught in a blizzard, it is not the government in London that feels cold. That is why the individual man is the bearer of good and evil, and not, on the one hand, any separate part of a man, or on the other hand, any collection of men. To believe that there can be good and evil in a collection of human beings, over and above the good or evil in the various individuals, is an error; moreover, it is an error which leads straight to totalitarianism, and is therefore dangerous.

There are some among philosophers and statesmen who think that the State can have an excellence of its own, and not merely as a means to the welfare of the citizens. I cannot see any reason to agree with this view. 'The State' is an abstraction; it does not feel pleasure or pain, it has no hopes or fears, and what we think of as its purposes are really the purposes of individuals who direct it. When we think concretely, not abstractly, we find, in place of 'the State', certain people who have more power than falls to the share of most men. And so glorification of 'the State' turns out to be, in fact, glorification of a governing minority. No democrat can tolerate such a fundamentally unjust theory.

There is another ethical theory, which to my mind is also inadequate; it is that which might be called the 'biological' theory, though I should not wish to assert that it is held by biologists. This view is derived from a contemplation of evolution. The struggle for existence is supposed to have gradually led to more and more complex organisms, culminating (so far) in man. In this view, survival is the supreme end, or rather, survival of one's own species. Whatever increases the human population of the globe, if this theory is right, is to count as 'good', and whatever diminishes the population is to count as 'bad'.

I cannot see any justification for such a mechanical and arithmetical outlook. It would be easy to find a single acre containing more ants than there are human beings in the whole world, but we do not on that account acknowledge the superior excellence of ants. And what human person would prefer a large population living in poverty and squalor to a smaller population living happily with a sufficiency of comfort?

It is true, of course, that survival is the necessary condition for everything else, but it is only a condition of what has value, and may have no value on its own account. Survival, in the world that modern science and technique have produced, demands a great deal of government. But what is to give value to survival must come mainly from sources that lie outside government. The reconciling of these two opposite requisites has been our problem in these discussions.

And now, gathering up the threads of our discussions, and remembering all the dangers of our time, I wish to reiterate certain conclusions, and, more particularly, to set forth the hopes which I believe we have rational grounds for entertaining.

Between those who care most for social cohesion and those who primarily value individual initiative there has been an age-long battle ever since the time of the ancient Greeks. In every such perennial controversy there is sure to be truth on both sides; there is not likely to be a clear-cut solution, but at best one involving various adjustments and compromises.

Throughout history, as I suggested in my second lecture, there has been a fluctuation between periods of excessive anarchy and periods of too strict governmental control. In our day, except (as yet) in the matter of world government, there has been too much tendency towards authority, and too little care for the preservation of initiative. Men in control of vast organisations have tended to be too abstract in their outlook, to forget what actual human beings are like, and to try to fit men to systems rather than systems to men.

The lack of spontaneity from which our highly organised societies tend to suffer is connected with excessive control over large areas by remote authorities.

One of the advantages to be gained from decentralisation is that it provides new opportunities for hopefulness and for individual activities that embody hopes. If our political thoughts are all concerned with vast problems and dangers of world catastrophe, it is easy to become despairing. Fear of war, fear of revolution, fear of reaction, may obsess you according to your temperament and your party bias. Unless you are one of a very small number of powerful individuals, you are likely to feel that you cannot do much about these great issues. But in relation to smaller problems – those of your town, or your trade union, or the local branch of your political party, for example – you can hope to have a successful influence. This will engender a hopeful spirit, and a hopeful spirit is what is most needed if a way is to be found of dealing successfully with the larger problems. War and shortages and financial stringency have caused almost universal fatigue, and have made hopefulness seem shallow and insincere. Success, even if, at first, it is on a small scale, is the best cure for this mood of pessimistic weariness. And success, for most people, means breaking up our problems, and being free to concentrate on those that are not too desperately large.

The world has become the victim of dogmatic political creeds, of which, in our day, the most powerful are capitalism and communism. I do not believe that either, in a dogmatic and unmitigated form, offers a cure for preventible evils. Capitalism gives opportunity of initiative to a few; communism could (though it does not in fact) provide a servile kind of security for all. But if people can rid themselves of the influence of unduly simple theories and the strife that they engender, it will be possible, by a wise use of scientific technique, to provide both opportunity for all and security for all. Unfortunately our political theories are less intelligent than our science, and we have not yet learnt how to make use of our knowledge and our skill in the ways that will do most to make life happy and even glorious. It is not only the experience and the fear of war that oppresses mankind, though this is perhaps the greatest of all the evils of our time. We are oppressed also by the great impersonal forces that govern our daily life, making us still slaves of circumstance though no longer slaves in law. This need not be the case. It has come about through the worship of false gods. Energetic men have worshipped power rather than simple happiness and friendliness; men of less energy have acquiesced, or have been deceived by a wrong diagnosis of the sources of sorrow.

Ever since mankind invented slavery, the powerful have believed that their happiness could be achieved by means that involved inflicting misery on others. Gradually, with the growth of democracy, and with the quite modern application of Christian ethics to politics and economics, a better ideal than that of the slave-holders has begun to prevail, and the claims of justice are now acknowledged as they never were at any former time. But in seeking justice by means of elaborate systems we have been in danger of forgetting that justice alone is not enough. Daily joys, times of liberation from care, adventure, and opportunity for creative activities, are at least as important as justice in bringing about a life that men can feel to be worth living. Monotony may be more deadening than an alternation of delight and agony. The men who think out administrative reforms and schemes of social amelioration are for the most part earnest men who are no longer young. Too often they have forgotten that to most people not only spontaneity but some kind of personal pride is necessary for happiness. The pride of a great conqueror is not one that a well-regulated world can allow, but the pride of the artist, of the discoverer, of the man who has turned a wilderness into a garden or has brought happiness where, but for him, there would have been misery – such pride is good, and our social system should make it possible, not only for the few, but for very many.

The instincts that long ago prompted the hunting and fighting activities of our savage ancestors demand an outlet; if they can find no other, they will turn to hatred and thwarted malice. But there are outlets for these very instincts that are not evil. For fighting it is possible to substitute emulation and active sport; for hunting, the joy of adventure and discovery and creation. We must not ignore these instincts, and we need not regret them; they are the source, not only of what is bad, but of what is best in human achievement. When security has been achieved, the most important task for those who seek human welfare will be to find for these ancient and powerful instincts neither merely restraints nor the outlets that make for destruction, but as many as possible of the outlets that give joy and pride and splendour to human life.

Throughout the ages of human development men have been subject to miseries of two kinds: those imposed by external nature, and those that human beings misguidedly inflicted upon each other. At first, by far the worst evils were those that were due to the environment. Man was a rare species, whose survival was precarious. Without the agility of the monkey, without any coating of fur, he had difficulty in escaping from wild beasts, and in most parts of the world could not endure the winter's cold. He had only two biological advantages: the upright posture freed his hands, and intelligence enabled him to transmit experience. Gradually these two advantages gave him supremacy. The numbers of the human species increased beyond those of any other large mammals. But nature could still assert her power by means of flood and famine and pestilence, and by exacting from the great majority of mankind incessant toil in the securing of daily bread.

In our own day our bondage to external nature is fast diminishing, as a result of the growth of scientific intelligence. Famines and pestilences still occur, but we know better, year by year, what should be done to prevent them. Hard work is still necessary, but only because we are unwise: given peace and co-operation, we could subsist on a very moderate amount of toil. With existing techniques, we can, whenever we choose to exercise wisdom, be free of many ancient forms of bondage to external nature.

But the evils that men inflict upon each other have not diminished in the same degree. There are still wars, oppressions, and hideous cruelties, and greedy men still snatch wealth from those who are less skilful or less ruthless than themselves. Love of power still leads to vast tyrannies, or to mere obstruction when its grosser forms are impossible. And fear – deep, scarcely conscious fear – is still the dominant motive in very many lives.

All this is unnecessary; there is nothing in human nature that makes these evils inevitable. I wish to repeat, with all possible emphasis, that I disagree completely with those who infer from our combative impulses that human nature demands war and other destructive forms of conflict. I firmly believe the very opposite of this. I maintain that combative impulses have an essential part to play, and in their harmful forms can be enormously lessened.

Greed of possession will grow less where there is no fear of destitution. Love of power can be satisfied in many ways that involve no injury to others: by the power over nature that results from discovery and invention, by the production of admired books or works of art, and by successful persuasion. Energy and the wish to be effective are beneficient if they can find the right outlet, and harmful if not − like steam, which can either drive the train or burst the boiler.

Our emancipation from bondage to external nature has made possible a greater degree of human well-being than has ever hitherto existed. But if this possibility is to be realised, there must be freedom of initiative in all ways not positively harmful, and encouragement of those forms of initiative that enrich the life of Man. We shall not create a good world by trying to make men tame and timid, but by encouraging them to be bold and adventurous and fearless except in inflicting injuries upon their fellow-men. In the world in which we find ourselves, the possibilities of good are almost limitless, and the possibilities of evil no less so. Our present predicament is due more than anything else to the fact that we have learnt to understand and control to a terrifying extent the forces of nature outside us, but not those that are embodied in ourselves. Self-control has always been a watchword of the moralists, but in the past it has been a control without understanding. In these lectures I have sought for a wider understanding of human needs than is assumed by most politicians and economists, for it is only through such an understanding that we can find our way to the realisation of those hopes which, though as yet they are largely frustrated by our folly, our skill has placed within our reach.

CPSIA information can be obtained
at www.ICGtesting.com
Printed in the USA
FFOW03n1253200817
38998FF